Study Guide

Study Guide

to accompany

ROBERT **SIEGLER**
JUDY **DELOACHE**
NANCY **EISENBERG**

How Children DEVELOP

Jill L. Saxon, Ph.D

WORTH PUBLISHERS

Study Guide
by Jill L. Saxon
to accompany
Siegler, DeLoache, Eisenberg: **How Children Develop**

Copyright © 2003 by Worth Publishers

ISBN: 1-57259-251-6

Printed in the United States of America

Printing: 5 4 3 2 1
Year: 06 05 04 03

Worth Publishers
41 Madison Avenue
New York, New York 10010
www.worthpublishers.com

Contents

Preface

This Study Guide is designed for use with *How Children Develop*, by Robert Siegler, Judy DeLoache, and Nancy Eisenberg. The 15 chapters correspond to the 15 chapters in the textbook. Each chapter contains a review section, two key term matching sections, multiple-choice questions, and essay questions. This book is intended to help students evaluate their understanding of the textbook material and then guide them toward any problem areas that need to be reviewed.

The first section in each chapter is entitled **"You Should Know."** Its purpose is to remind students of the general content areas of the textbook, including both factual and conceptual issues. Rather than duplicating the summary sections located in the text book, the "You Should Know" section helps students organize their knowledge in a series of "hows," "whys," and "whats" presented in a bullet-point style.

Each chapter also contains two **key term matching sections**. Key Term Matching I allows students to test their knowledge of the key terms and their definitions in the traditional fashion. Key Term Matching II allows students to assess their knowledge of key terms with a more difficult test of concepts, by pairing key terms with appropriate applications and examples.

The **Multiple-Choice Questions** section contains 20 sample multiple-choice items that are designed to be similar in style and content to those items students will find on quizzes and exams. The questions vary as to difficulty level and test both definitional and conceptual knowledge. Some items concentrate on direct recall of information, while other items require a deeper understanding of the material and the ability to apply the concepts to real-world examples.

An **answer key** containing answers to the two matching sections and the multiple-choice questions appears at the end of each chapter.

Finally, each chapter contains five sample **essay questions**, again designed to be similar in style and content to questions students may find on quizzes and exams. The essay questions vary in their requirements, from a simple review of material to applications of concepts.

I am grateful to Worth Publishers and to Robert Siegler, Judy DeLoache, and Nancy Eisenberg for the opportunity to work with them on this endeavor. The textbook authors provided guidance throughout the project and placed a great deal of importance on its quality. I would like to thank my editors, Marge Byers, Graig Donini, Eve Conte, Tim Robinson, and Stacey Alexander, for their encouragement and support throughout the project.

I hope students find this Study Guide valuable and are able to use it as an integral part of their study and review plan. I welcome any suggestions for improvement.

JLS

CHAPTER 1
An Introduction to Child Development

You Should Know:

Introduction

- how Werner's Kauai study was unique and what it demonstrated about the influence of biological and environmental factors.

Why Study Child Development? (*summary on pg. 7 of text*)

Raising Children
- how child-development research can inform parents and teachers.

Choosing Social Policies
- how child-development research can inform social policy.
- how child-development research led to a different understanding of the factors involved in children's testimonies in legal settings.

Understanding Human Nature
- how child-development research can help us better understand human nature in general.

Historical Foundations of the Study of Child Development (*summary on pg. 9 of text*)

Early Philosophical Views of Children's Development
- what Plato, Aristotle, Locke, and Rousseau thought about children, whether they possessed innate knowledge, and how they should be disciplined, as well as on what these views were based.

The Beginnings of Research on Children
- what sparked the research-based approach to understanding child development.
- how Freud's and Watson's theories were an improvement over those of their predecessors, although they were too limited.

Enduring Themes in Child Development (*summary on pg. 24 of text*)

1. Nature and Nurture

- what is meant by nature and what is meant by nurture.
- what types of questions researchers generally ask about the influences of nature and nurture.
- how research on adolescence has demonstrated the influences of both nature and nurture.

Box 1.1: The Importance of Normal Early Experience

- what research on Romanian orphans has demonstrated about the importance of early experience.

2. The Active Child

- what is meant by "the active child" and the general ways children influence their own development.
- how children's contribution to their own development changes with age.

3. Continuity/Discontinuity

- what is meant by continuous development and discontinuous development.
- how the continuity of development can differ depending on one's perspective.

4. Mechanisms of Developmental Change

- how the evolutionary perspective has provided a useful framework for thinking about how change occurs.

5. The Sociocultural Context

- what is meant by the sociocultural context and what methods researchers generally use to examine the impact of the sociocultural context.
- what this research has demonstrated about the effect of family sleeping arrangements on children.
- how the sociocultural context can vary within a particular culture and across cultures.

6. Individual Differences

- the sources of individual differences, especially among members of the same family.

7. Research and Children's Welfare

- how an understanding of child development can lead to practical benefits for children.
- how this understanding has led to benefits for children in the visual and learning domains.

Methods for Studying Child Development (*summary on pg. 37 of text*)

The Scientific Method

- the basic assumption and steps of the scientific method, and how this differs from prior methods.
- the key properties of good scientific measures.

Contexts for Gathering Data About Children

- what the three main contexts for gathering information about children are, as well as examples of research using these contexts.
- what each context offers researchers in terms of the information they can collect, as well as the disadvantages of each context.

Correlation and Causation

- the goals of studies using correlational designs and experimental designs.
- what a correlation is, and the characteristics of the correlation coefficient.
- what a correlation can tell you and what it cannot tell you.
- the logic behind experimental designs and random assignments.
- the types of groups and variables in an experimental design.
- the advantages and disadvantages of experimental designs and how naturalistic experiments overcome some of these limitations.

Designs for Examining Development

- the characteristics of cross-sectional, longitudinal, and microgenetic designs, with examples of each.
- the goals and advantages of these three designs, as well as their limitations.

Ethical Issues in Child-Development Research

- the important aspects of the ethical code for research with children.

Key Term Matching I: Definitions

Instructions: Match each key term with its definition.

Set A

KEY TERM

1. _____ hypotheses	11. _____ independent variable
2. _____ correlation	12. _____ internal validity
3. _____ dependent variable	13. _____ experimental group
4. _____ interrater reliability	14. _____ nature
5. _____ correlation coefficient	15. _____ selection
6. _____ variation	16. _____ nurture
7. _____ variables	17. _____ test-retest reliability
8. _____ control group	18. _____ scientific method
9. _____ third-variable problem	19. _____ external validity
10. _____ direction-of-causation problem	

DEFINITION

a. the degree to which the results of research can be generalized beyond the particular children and methods used in the study

b. the experience children in the experimental group receive and children in the control group do not receive

c. the environments, both physical and social, that influence development

d. the more frequent survival and reproduction of organisms that are well-adapted to their environment

e. an approach to testing beliefs that involves choosing a question, formulating a hypothesis, testing the hypothesis, and drawing a conclusion

f. a statistic that indicates the direction and strength of the association between two variables

g. the degree to which different observers of the same behavior agree

h. the degree to which children's performance on two or more occasions is similar

i.   the degree to which the effects observed in experiments can be attributed to the variables that the researcher intentionally manipulated

j.   one's biological endowment; in particular, the genes received from one's parents

k.   attributes that vary across individuals and situations

l.   the association between two variables

m.   educated guesses

n.   the notion that correlations do not indicate which variable, if either, is the cause of the other

o.   the notion that a correlation between two variables could result from both variables being influenced by another, unspecified variable

p.   a group of children in an experimental design that is presented with the experience that is of interest to the researcher

q.   the group of children in an experimental design given an experience identical to that of children in the experimental group, except that they are not presented with the experience of interest to the researcher

r.   differences within and among individuals

s.   a behavior that is hypothesized to be affected by the experience of interest to the researcher

Set B

KEY TERM

20. _____ validity
21. _____ naturalistic experiments
22. _____ clinical interview
23. _____ discontinuous development
24. _____ correlational designs
25. _____ structured interview
26. _____ microgenetic design
27. _____ stage theories
28. _____ longitudinal design
29. _____ experimental designs

30. _____ naturalistic observation
31. _____ experimental control
32. _____ cross-sectional design
33. _____ continuous development
34. _____ structured observation
35. _____ reliability
36. _____ socioeconomic status
37. _____ random assignment
38. _____ sociocultural context

DEFINITION

t. approaches to development that propose development occurs in a series of distinct age-related steps

u. the notion that changes with age occur in sudden, large shifts

v. a method of study in which the same children are studied repeatedly over a short period of time

w. a procedure in which the questions are modified according to participants' responses

x. a measure of social class based on education and income

y. the degree to which independent measurements of a behavior are consistent

z. the degree to which a test measures what it intends to measure

aa. a research method in which all participants are asked the same questions

bb. the notion that changes with age occur gradually

cc. examination of children's behaviors in their usual environments

dd. examination of children's behaviors in an environment where all participants are presented with identical situations

ee. the physical, social, cultural, economic, and historical circumstances that make up a child's environment

ff. studies that allow researchers to make inferences about causes and effects

gg.   a procedure that gives each participant an equal chance of being selected for each group within an experiment

hh.   the ability of the researcher to determine the specific experiences that children in each group encounter during the study

ii.   a type of experimental design in which data are collected in everyday settings rather than in a laboratory

jj.   a research method in which children of different ages are compared on a particular behavior or characteristic

kk.   a research method in which the same children are studied two or more times over a substantial period of time

ll.   studies designed to indicate how variables are related to each other

Key Term Matching II: Applications, Examples, and More

Instructions: Match each key term with an application or example of the term.

Set A

KEY TERM

1. _____ test-retest reliability
2. _____ selection
3. _____ interrater reliability
4. _____ dependent variable
5. _____ nature
6. _____ internal validity
7. _____ third-variable problem
8. _____ control group
9. _____ independent variable

10. _____ scientific method
11. _____ hypotheses
12. _____ experimental group
13. _____ nurture
14. _____ correlation coefficient
15. _____ external validity
16. _____ variables
17. _____ variation
18. _____ direction-of-causation problem

APPLICATION OR EXAMPLE

a. what differentiates this from past approaches is research methods yield higher-quality evidence allowing for more solid conclusions

b. examples of these are socioeconomic status, marital status, IQ, and number of friends

c. the variety of strategies or behaviors an individual has for a particular task is considered

d. this process involves choosing from among a variety of behaviors or strategies the one that allows individuals to meet their goals consistently, quickly, and easily

e. although one can control one's environment to some extent, one has no control over the influence of this on development

f. if both marital conflict and sibling conflict are caused by a family's poor economic circumstances, then a correlation between the two types of conflict would have this

g. a measure of children's school achievement would be considered to have poor _____ if two teachers demonstrated low levels of agreement on the measure

h.   a measure of children's school achievement would be considered to have high _____ if children who do well on it at one point in time also do well on it later and children who do poorly at one point in time also do poorly on it later

i.   if a researcher provides social skills training to children entering first grade and then observes that they have more friends after the training than before, the mere passage of time may be an explanation for a lack of this

j.   finding the same results in multiple studies, conducted with different children in different schools and socioeconomic classes and using a variety of methods, establishes the _____ of the findings

k.   the prenatal environment (e.g., poor oxygen in utero as a result of maternal smoking) is considered to be part of this type of influence

l.   when this number is high and negative, as in minus .67, it means the knowledge that an individual's score is high on one variable will suggest that that his or her score will be low on the other variable

m.   a person who concludes a strong correlation between marital conflict and sibling conflict indicates that marital conflict causes sibling conflict, when it could be vice-versa, is demonstrating this

n.   these might include, "Children who have a greater number of classmates will develop better social skills," for the research question, "How does the number of children in a classroom relate to children's social skills?"

o.   in a study of the effects of social skills training on friendship formation, the children who receive such training comprise this

p.   in a study about the effects of social skills training on friendship formation, the children who do not receive the training but are treated identically otherwise are in this

q.   in a study about the effects of social skills training on friendship formation, the training is referred to as this

r.   in a study about the effects of social skills training on friendship formation, the number of friends formed following the training is referred to as this

Set B

KEY TERM

19. _____ discontinuous development   27. _____ correlational designs

20. _____ longitudinal design   28. _____ validity

21. _____ structured observation   29. _____ microgenetic design

22. _____ clinical interview   30. _____ reliability

23. _____ cross-sectional design   31. _____ stage theories

24. _____ experimental designs   32. _____ random assignment

25. _____ continuous development   33. _____ naturalistic observation

26. _____ structured interview   34. _____ naturalistic experiments

APPLICATION OR EXAMPLE

s.   a study in which researchers examine the change in level of sibling conflict after some sibling pairs are taught strategies to decrease conflict while other sibling pairs receive no training is using one of these

t.   a study in which children are asked a series of 10 prepared questions about their sibling relationships is using this method

u.   this method is specifically designed to provide an in-depth depiction of the processes that involve change

v.   this criterion for a good measure could also be referred to as consistency

w.   these still employ random assignment, but have greater external validity than laboratory experiments do

x.   stage theories support the idea of this type of development

y.   a study in which children are probed as to their feelings about their siblings by a researcher who deviates from the script to adjust to particular children's responses is using this method

z.   a study in which children's sibling relationships are examined by mounting unobtrusive cameras throughout their home is using this method

aa.   a study in which children's sibling relationships are examined by bringing sibling pairs into the laboratory and asking them to complete a series of puzzles is using this method

bb.   a study in which the researcher examines the association between marital conflict and sibling rivalry is using one of these

cc.   a focus on the large differences between children of different ages, such as the difference between a nonverbal infant and a preschooler who speaks in complete sentences, may lead to a view that is in <u>opposition</u> to the idea of this type of development

dd.   the logic behind this procedure is that groups created in this manner should be comparable on any variable at the beginning of the experiment

ee.   this criterion for a good measure of marital conflict would not be met if children are asked to rate the degree of conflict between their parents as some parents score low simply because they argue only behind closed doors

ff.   a study in which children who are two-, four-, six-, and eight-year-olds are simultaneously compared on the number of words in their vocabulary is utilizing this

gg.   a study in which children are followed from the age of two to eight and the number of words in their vocabulary is examined every two years is utilizing this

hh.   Piaget's theory of cognitive development, Freud's theory of psychosexual development, and Kohlberg's theory of moral development are all these

Multiple-Choice Questions

1. Werner's Kauai study demonstrated which of the following?
   A. Some biological disadvantages lead only to long-term negative outcomes if there are also environmental disadvantages.
   B. Some biological disadvantages cannot be overcome by environmental advantages.
   C. Some environmental disadvantages cannot be overcome by biological advantages.
   D. all of the above

2. Which of the following historical figures did not emphasize the importance of early discipline but did emphasize the importance of giving children the greatest amount of freedom?
   A. Aristotle
   B. Locke
   C. Plato
   D. Rousseau

3. Watson based his theory of child development in large part on which of the following?
   A. hypnosis and analysis of dreams and childhood memories
   B. systematic daily diary of a single child's growth
   C. experiments on reward and punishment of rats and other animals
   D. study of children working in coal mines

4. The finding that children who grow up in troubled homes are more likely than other children to become schizophrenic is evidence of:
   A. the influence of nature.
   B. the influence of nurture.
   C. the interaction of nature and nurture.
   D. random variation in the population.

5. Which of the following evidence would provide the most support for the influence of nature on the development of empathy?
   A. In comparison with other adopted children, the only children who show high levels of empathy are those whose biological parents are empathetic and who grow up with caring and altruistic parents.
   B. Children who grow up with caring and altruistic parents are more likely than other children to be empathetic, even when adopted as infants.
   C. Children whose biological parents are empathetic are more likely than other children to be empathetic, even when adopted as infants.
   D. There is no association between parents' characteristics and children's empathy.

6. The "active" child refers to which of the following?
   A. children whose environments impact their development
   B. children as shapers of their own development
   C. children who have been diagnosed with attention deficit hyperactivity disorder
   D. children whose biology affects their development

7. Which of the following does not belong with the others?
   A. discontinuous
   B. stage
   C. gradual
   D. qualitatively different

8. Which of the following is <u>not</u> generally considered to constitute part of the sociocultural context of a child's life?
   A. the price of milk
   B. child abuse laws
   C. intelligence of child
   D. school teachers' training

9. Children with specific language impairment were assisted by research on:
   A. individual differences.
   B. successive approximation.
   C. preferential looking.
   D. sociocultural context.

10. Which of the following is <u>not</u> one of the four steps of the scientific method?
   A. drawing a conclusion
   B. publishing research so parents and educators can benefit from it
   C. developing a method to test the hypothesis
   D. choosing a question

11. Which of the following indicates that a measure of preschoolers' peer acceptance has poor reliability?
   A. Teacher A and Teacher B disagree about which children are liked and which are disliked.
   B. Children's reports on one day of who they like and dislike differ from their reports the following day.
   C. Researchers' counts of how many times a child is asked to play a game are unrelated to how much other children say they like that child.
   D. A and B
   E. all of the above

12. To examine the effectiveness of empathy training on children's sharing behavior, two months of training is provided to three-year-old children living in rural Georgia. Six months later, the children's sharing behaviors are measured and compared to their pre-training sharing behavior. Improvements are considered the result of the empathy training. Which of the following is a potential source of external invalidity?
   A. All children were from rural Georgia.
   B. The observers of the sharing behavior may disagree with each other.
   C. Children's sharing behavior may improve with the simple passage of time.
   D. Children who were the best sharers before the training were not necessarily the best after the training.

13. A clinical interview would probably be the method of choice for a researcher interested in:
   A. how young children negotiate with each other when there is only a single desirable toy.
   B. the frequency of sexual harassment behavior among adolescents.
   C. the extent to which the children in an elementary school class like to play with each other.
   D. obtaining extensive information about a single child's feelings about his friendships.

14. Which of the following is a disadvantage of structured observation?
   A. Memory of participants for past events is often inaccurate and incomplete.
   B. It is difficult to isolate the aspects of the situation that are most influential.
   C. Reports are often biased to reflect favorably on the participants.
   D. It has a limited value for studying infrequent behaviors.
   E. none of the above

15. Variables X and Y are positively correlated. This correlation indicates which of the following?
   A. As the level of X increases, the level of Y decreases.
   B. As the level of Y increases, the level of X decreases.
   C. As the level of Y increases, the level of X increases.
   D. As the level of X decreases, the level of Y decreases.
   E. A and B
   F. C and D

16. A correlation coefficient of +.80 indicates that, as the level of one variable increases, the level of the other variable:
   A. increases.
   B. decreases.
   C. stays the same.
   D. varies randomly.

17. The direction-of-causation problem refers to the fact that:
   A. experimental designs cannot specify cause and effect.
   B. a correlation does not indicate which variable is the cause and which is the effect.
   C. researchers often mistake negative correlations for positive ones.
   D. the correlation between two variables might be caused by an unspecified variable.

18. A class of third-grade children is split into two groups through random assignment. Group A is given training in a new game and Group B is not. Both groups are then tested on their skill in playing the new game. We consider Group A to be the _____ group and Group B to be the _____ group.
   A. dependent; independent
   B. independent; dependent
   C. control; experimental
   D. experimental; control

19. Which of the following could <u>not</u> be examined with an experimental design?
   A. effect of physical attractiveness on children's school grades
   B. effect of amount of homework on teenage drinking behavior
   C. effect of TV violence on preschoolers' aggressive behavior
   D. effect of parental discipline practices on children's peer relations

20. A researcher interested in the development of reading skills follows a group of children from ages six to ten. Every six months, children are given a reading test. This researcher is using which type of design?
   A. experimental
   B. correlational
   C. longitudinal
   D. cross-sectional

Essay Questions

Instructions: Answer the following essay questions on a separate sheet of paper.

1. Describe the biological and environmental factors you believe influence the development of walking. In your discussion of this topic, be sure to think about the following questions: Are there any biological factors that you believe are unaffected by environment (exert their influence regardless of the environment)? Are there any environmental factors that you believe are unaffected by biology (exert their influence regardless of biology)? In contrast, are there biological factors that can exert an influence only in particular environments? Are there any environmental factors that can exert an influence only when particular biological characteristics are present?

2. Rachel is a six-month-old who has just learned to sit up on her own. Her mother places two toys in front of her, a soft yellow stuffed animal within her reach and a colorful rattle slightly out of her reach. Seeing both toys, Rachel chooses the one she is more interested in playing. Over time, Rachel makes many such choices among a variety of objects. From the perspective of children as active participants in their own development, describe three examples of how Rachel's choices of toys to play with may impact her development. You may think about the development of motor skills, likes and dislikes, the understanding of the way different objects function, or any other aspects of development you think may be influenced by choices such as these.

3. Describe how variation and selection might function in the development of the ability to complete puzzles.

4. A researcher is interested in examining sex differences in children's ability to join a group of peers already playing a game. Design two studies to examine this issue, one using structured observation and the other using naturalistic observation. Describe the advantages and disadvantages of each method.

5. Imagine you are a researcher interested in developmental changes in children's strategies for getting others to share. Briefly describe how you could examine this using each of the following designs: (a) cross-sectional, (b) longitudinal, and (c) microgenetic. For each design, be sure to indicate what research question you would be addressing.

Answer Key

Key Term Matching I

1. m	7. k	13. p	19. a	25. aa	31. hh	37. gg
2. l	8. q	14. j	20. z	26. v	32. jj	38. ee
3. s	9. o	15. d	21. ii	27. t	33. bb	
4. g	10. n	16. c	22. w	28. kk	34. dd	
5. f	11. b	17. h	23. u	29. ff	35. y	
6. r	12. i	18. e	24. ll	30. cc	36. x	

Key Term Matching II

1. h	6. i	11. n	16. b	21. aa	26. t	31. hh
2. d	7. f	12. o	17. c	22. y	27. bb	32. dd
3. g	8. p	13. k	18. m	23. ff	28. ee	33. z
4. r	9. q	14. l	19. x	24. s	29. u	34. w
5. e	10. a	15. j	20. gg	25. cc	30. v	

Multiple-Choice Questions

1. A	6. B	11. D	16. A
2. D	7. C	12. A	17. B
3. C	8. C	13. D	18. D
4. B	9. B	14. E	19. A
5. C	10. B	15. F	20. C

CHAPTER 2
Prenatal Development, Birth, and the Newborn Period

You Should Know:

Prenatal Development (*summary on pg. 66 of text*)

Introduction
- how modern scientific techniques have changed the view of prenatal development.

Box 2.1: Beng Beginnings
- how cultural beliefs about when life begins can underlie childrearing beliefs and practices.

Conception
- how sperm and egg are formed.
- how conception occurs and what it involves.
- what occurs during the three periods of prenatal development, beginning with conception.

Box 2.2: The First Sex Differences
- the differences between males and females in their rates of their conception, miscarriage, and survival, as well as in their vulnerability to developmental disorders.
- how sociocultural context can influence the differential survival of males and females.

Developmental Processes
- the four major developmental processes that underlie the transformation of a zygote into an embryo and then into a fetus.
- how the flexibility of cells changes as they develop.

Box 2.3: Phylogenetic Continuity
- the rationale behind analogies made between humans and other animals.

Early Development
- how different types of twins originate.
- how the zygote transforms into an embryo.
- the functions of the components of the embryo's support system.

An Illustrated Summary of Prenatal Development
- the general order in which development proceeds.

Fetal Behavior
- how the fetus plays an active role in its own physical and behavioral development.
- the types and functions of movements common to the fetus.
- how fetal states are associated with newborn states.

Fetal Experience
- what the fetus experiences in terms of touch, taste, smell, hearing, and sight.
- how research has demonstrated fetal sensory experience.

Fetal Learning
- what evidence exists for fetuses learning from experiences in the womb.
- how newborn preferences are associated with prenatal experiences.
- what fetuses are probably *unable* to learn.

Hazards to Prenatal Development
- what environmental agents can pose harm to the developing organism and how these agents affect the fetus.
- how the timing and amount of exposure, as well as individual fetal differences, are related to the effect of the agent on the developing organism.
- how maternal factors, such as stress and age, can influence prenatal development.

Box 2.4: Face Up to Wake Up
- what SIDS is and how it can best be prevented.

The Birth Experience (*summary on pg. 69 of text*)

Introduction
- how the birth process itself serves an adaptive function for the newborn.

Diversity of Childbirth Practices
- how childbirth practices can vary according to cultural values and goals.

The Newborn Infant (*summary on pg. 79 of text*)

State of Arousal

- the pattern and adaptive significance of newborn states and how and why these change with development.
- how infants' state can influence their experience of the world as well as parent-infant interactions.
- how and when caregivers should respond to infant crying.

Negative Outcomes at Birth

- how and why infant mortality rates differ across countries and subcultures of the United States.
- the causes and consequences of low birth weight and how intervention programs have been successful and unsuccessful.
- how risk factors tend to co-occur, how vulnerability is associated with the number of risk factors a baby has, and how socioeconomic status relates to risk factors.
- the factors associated with developmental resilience.

Box 2.5: Parenting a Low-Birth-Weight Baby

- how and why parenting a low-birth-weight baby is more challenging than parenting normal-weight babies and what parents can do for help.

Key Term Matching I: Definitions

Instructions: Match each key term with its definition.

Set A

KEY TERM

1. _____ amniotic sac
2. _____ fetal alcohol syndrome
3. _____ dose-response relation
4. _____ blastocyst
5. _____ neural tube
6. _____ low birth weight
7. _____ umbilical cord
8. _____ embryo
9. _____ sudden infant death syndrome
10. _____ premature
11. _____ placenta
12. _____ colic
13. _____ teratogens
14. _____ small for gestational age
15. _____ sensitive period
16. _____ inner cell mass
17. _____ zygote

DEFINITION

a.   the unexpected death of an infant that has no identifiable cause

b.   the period of time during which a developing organism is most at risk for harm from outside agents

c.   babies that weigh substantially less than normal for their gestational age

d.   the organ rich with blood vessels that permits the exchange of materials between the bloodstreams of the mother and the fetus

e.   the bulge of cells (inside the hollow sphere of cells) that eventually forms into the embryo

f.   the groove formed in the embryo that will eventually develop into its brain and spinal cord

g.   a birth weight less than 5.5 lbs.

h.   a developing organism in its 3rd to 8th week of prenatal development

i.   the fact that the likelihood and severity of a prenatal defect occurring as a result of teratogen exposure is associated with the level of exposure to the teratogen

j.   excessive crying occurring in the first few months of life that occurs for no apparent reason

k.   the membrane that is filled with a clear, watery fluid in which the fetus floats

l.   a condition caused by prenatal exposure to alcohol

m.   the fertilized egg

n.   the tube that contains the blood vessels running between the mother and the fetus

o.   the hollow sphere of cells into which the zygote arranges itself

p.   a child born at or before 35 weeks following conception

q.   environmental agents that can cause harm to the developing organism

Set B

KEY TERM

18. _____ conception

19. _____ swaddling

20. _____ identical twins

21. _____ state

22. _____ phylogenic continuity

23. _____ non-REM sleep

24. _____ habituation

25. _____ developmental resilience

26. _____ cephalocaudal development

27. _____ epigenesis

28. _____ apoptosis

29. _____ fraternal twins

30. _____ autostimulation theory

31. _____ embryology

32. _____ gastrulation

33. _____ gametes

34. _____ REM

35. _____ meiosis

DEFINITION

r.   the process by which the inner cell mass becomes the embryo and the rest of the cells become its support system

s.   an infant's level of arousal and engagement in the environment

t.   a form of learning that involves a decrease in response to repeated stimulation

u.   cell death that is programmed

v.   the notion that brain activity during REM sleep facilitates the early development of the visual system in the fetus and newborn

w.   cell division process that results in cells containing only half of the normal set of chromosomes

x.   a quiet or deep sleep characterized by the absence of motor activity and eye movements

y.   the union of sperm and egg

z.   an active sleep state characterized by quick, jerky eye movements

aa.   the notion that humans share some characteristics and developmental processes with other animals as a result of our common evolutionary history

bb.   a soothing technique which involves wrapping an infant tightly in a blanket

cc.   siblings that result when the zygote splits in half

dd.   successful development occurring in the face of multiple developmental hazards

ee.   the emergence of new structures and functions during development ff.   sperm and egg

gg.   the pattern of growth in which areas near the head develop earlier than areas farther away from the head

hh.   the study of prenatal development

ii.   siblings that result when two eggs released into the fallopian tube at the same time are fertilized by two sperm

Key Term Matching II: Applications, Examples, and More

Instructions: Match each key term with an application or example of the term.

Set A

KEY TERM

1. _____ colic
2. _____ neural tube
3. _____ sensitive period
4. _____ low birth weight
5. _____ fetal alcohol syndrome
6. _____ umbilical cord
7. _____ blastocyst
8. _____ teratogens
9. _____ sudden infant death syndrome

10. _____ inner cell mass
11. _____ small for gestational age
12. _____ zygote
13. _____ placenta
14. _____ premature
15. _____ amniotic sac
16. _____ embryo
17. _____ dose-response relation

APPLICATION OR EXAMPLE

a.   symptoms of this include facial deformities, mental retardation, and organ defects

b.   this encapsulates the inner cell mass

c.   this organ allows oxygen, nutrients, and minerals to pass from the mother to the developing organism, but does not allow their blood to mix

d.   a baby born at 34 weeks following conception who weighs 6.5 lbs. is this

e.   the amount and length of exposure to potentially harmful environmental agents is crucial in determining the effect of exposure because of this

f.   a baby born full-term who weighs less than is normal is considered to be of low birth weight <u>and</u> this

g.   cell division begins during this period of prenatal development

h.   fusion of the U-shaped groove in the top layer of the differentiated inner cell mass forms this

i.   as a result of this, <u>only</u> babies who were exposed to thalidomide while the limbs were emerging and developing were born with major limb deformities

j.   babies with this are more likely to suffer from hearing, language, and cognitive impairments, as well as a variety of social problems

k.   this part of the zygote folds itself into three layers

l.   this contains the fluid that cushions the developing organism from jolts

m.   the inner cell mass differentiates into three layers during this period of prenatal development

n.   these include legal and illegal drugs, as well as environmental pollutants such as mercury

o.   the risk of this is decreased by putting babies to sleep on their backs

p.   this tube runs between the placenta and the fetus

q.   this may cause parents to feel inadequate in their ability to soothe their baby

Set B

KEY TERM

18. _____ non-REM sleep	27. _____ developmental resilience
19. _____ fraternal twins	28. _____ conception
20. _____ phylogenic continuity	29. _____ gastrulation
21. _____ embryology	30. _____ state
22. _____ identical twins	31. _____ meiosis
23. _____ autostimulation theory	32. _____ habituation
24. _____ apoptosis	33. _____ REM
25. _____ epigenesis	34. _____ gametes
26. _____ cephalocaudal development	35. _____ swaddling

APPLICATION OR EXAMPLE

r.   this points out the high degree of brain activity during REM sleep as it tries to explain newborns' high levels of active sleep

s.   this is a rejection of the idea of preformation

t.   this may help make up for the little visual stimulation experienced by fetuses and newborns

u.   the result of this is a zygote

v.   following this process, the embryo is differentiated from its support system

w.   this is the study of physical and behavioral development in the womb

x.   this technique restricts the limb movement of the infant

y.   this affects young infants' experience of the world and can range from deep sleep to intense activity

z.   this pattern explains why the hands develop before the feet

aa.   this process produces sperm and eggs

bb.   twins who share half of their genetic material

cc.   this principle enables research on fetal exposure to alcohol conducted with mice to be applicable to humans

dd.   these cells are formed by meiosis

ee.   children who demonstrate this often have a responsive caregiver and personal characteristics such as intelligence and a sense of being capable of achieving their goals

ff.   an example of this is the death of cells in between the ridges in the hand plate of the developing organism

gg.   this is one of the simplest forms of learning and was demonstrated when fetuses were repeatedly presented with a recording of the sound "babi"

hh.   siblings with the exact same genetic makeup

ii.   this is characterized by slow brain waves, breathing, and heart rate

Multiple-Choice Questions

1. The study of prenatal development is referred to as:
   A. prenatology.
   B. developmental psychology.
   C. embryology.
   D. meiosis.

2. The union of sperm and egg is termed:
   A. mating.
   B. conception.
   C. meiosis.
   D. apoptosis.

3. Which of the following is an example of cell migration?
   A. splitting of the fertilized egg into two equal parts
   B. death of cells in between the ridges on the hand plate
   C. movement of new cells into the outer layer of the brain
   D. specialization of eye cells

4. The study in which cells located in the eye region of a frog embryo were moved to its belly demonstrated which of the following about cells transplanted early versus later in development?
   A. Cells transplanted early became a <u>normal part</u> of the belly, but those transplanted later became an <u>eye</u> lodged in the belly.
   B. Cells transplanted early became an <u>eye</u> lodged in the belly, but those transplanted later became a <u>normal part</u> of the belly.
   C. The cells became a <u>normal part</u> of the belly no matter whether they were transplanted early or late in development.
   D. The cells became an <u>eye</u> lodged in the belly no matter whether they were transplanted early or late in development.

5. Fraternal twins originate:
   A. when an inner cell mass splits in half.
   B. when an embryo splits in half.
   C. from two eggs being fertilized by two sperm.
   D. when an egg splits and is fertilized by two sperm.

6. Which of the following is <u>not</u> part of the fetus' support system?
   A. umbilical cord
   B. amniotic sac
   C. placenta
   D. neural tube

7. What causes fetal hiccups?
A. The fetus swallows air.
B. The mother's hiccups are transmitted across the placenta.
C. The fetus' grasping of the umbilical cord restricts airflow to the fetus.
D. The cause is unknown.

8. A fetus' activity level while in the uterus is _____ over time, and/but it is _____ to postnatal activity level.
A. consistent; unrelated
B. consistent; related
C. inconsistent; unrelated
D. inconsistent; related

9. Which of the following is a true statement about fetus' auditory (hearing) experiences during the last few months of the pregnancy?
A. The fetus' auditory organs are so underdeveloped before birth that it does not have the ability to hear.
B. The fetus' auditory organs are sufficiently developed to hear, but the amniotic fluid muffles all noises so greatly that the fetus cannot hear anything.
C. The fetus' auditory organs are sufficiently developed to hear, and the fetus can hear many, but not all, features of internal and external sounds.
D. The fetus' auditory organs are sufficiently developed to hear, and thus the fetus can hear internal and external noises almost perfectly.

10. Which of the following is evidence that a fetus has habituated to a repeated stimulus?
A. decreased changes in heart rate
B. turning towards a stimulus
C. increased changes in heart rate
D. increased movement

11. Rhonda is pregnant with twins, Fetus A and Fetus B. She is caught in traffic, and there are car horns blaring every few moments. Both fetuses initially experience a heart rate deceleration. As the car horn blaring continues, however, both fetuses' heart rate response decreases. After several minutes, a church bell rings loudly. The heart rate of Fetus A changes, but the heart rate of Fetus B does not change. Which of the following is <u>not</u> a possible explanation for the differences in the responses of the twin fetuses?
A. Fetus A heard the church bell, whereas Fetus B did not.
B. Fetus A learned to recognize the sound of the horns, whereas Fetus B did not.
C. Fetus A recognized the difference between the sounds of the car horns and the church bell, whereas Fetus B did not.
D. All of the above are possible explanations.

12. Which of the following is <u>not</u> a true statement about newborn preferences?
    A. Newborns prefer to listen to their mother's voice over another woman's voice.
    B. Newborns prefer to smell their own amniotic fluid over another baby's amniotic fluid.
    C. Newborns prefer to taste foods their mother ate while they were in the womb over other foods.
    D. Newborns prefer to hear novel sound patterns, such as poems and songs, over sound patterns they heard in the womb.

13. The sensitive period of the majority of major organ systems occurs in which period of prenatal development?
    A. embryonic
    B. fetal
    C. zygotic
    D. The sensitive period occurs dispersed throughout the entire prenatal period.

14. Which of the following has negative effects on prenatal development?
    A. cigarette smoke
    B. alcohol
    C. cocaine
    D. all of the above

15. It is difficult to isolate the effects of severe emotional stress on prenatal development because it often coincides with which of the following?
    A. SIDS
    B. exposure to environmental pollutants
    C. alcohol consumption
    D. rubella

16. Most newborn infants spend the majority of their day in which of the following states?
    A. autostimulation
    B. sleep
    C. crying
    D. awake alert

17. Which of the following is the best explanation for the large amount of time newborns spend in REM sleep?
    A. Newborns just sleep a lot overall.
    B. The brain activity generated during REM sleep partially compensates for the relatively little visual stimulation newborns receive throughout the day.
    C. Newborns have immature nervous systems.
    D. The neurotransmitter production accomplished during REM sleep causes newborns to cry when they need food.

18. Wrapping a baby tightly in clothes or a blanket is referred to as:
  A. swaddling.
  B. swanking.
  C. swapping.
  D. squeezing.

19. In the poor areas of the city in northeast Brazil that was described in the text where the infant mortality rate is as high as 90%, the infants who are most likely to survive may be those who:
  A. are extremely fatigued and sleep a lot.
  B. are patient and quiet.
  C. cry a lot.
  D. display evidence of malnutrition.

20. A multiple-risk model of prenatal and later development states that multiple risks are likely to:
  A. be cumulative.
  B. counteract each other.
  C. encourage resiliency.
  D. B and C

Essay Questions

Instructions: Answer the following essay questions on a separate sheet of paper.

1. Describe the following components of the fetal support system: placenta, umbilical cord, and amniotic sac. For each component, explain what it is as well as what its functions are.

2. Design a study to examine whether 35-week-old fetuses can differentiate between high-pitched melodies and low-pitched melodies. Be specific as to your methodology and what results you would expect if fetuses are able to differentiate between the melodies of different pitches. Then, describe how you could also examine whether the fetuses remembered the melodies over the course of a week. What would the results look like if fetuses were able to remember the melodies?

3. Describe three examples of newborn preferences that are based on prenatal experience.

4. Describe how cultural beliefs and practices can influence the child birth process and treatment of the newborn.

5. Describe what it means when psychologists say that infant crying has adaptive significance.

Answer Key

Key Term Matching I

1. k	6. g	11. d	16. e	21. s	26. gg	31. hh
2. l	7. n	12. j	17. m	22. aa	27. ee	32. r
3. i	8. h	13. q	18. y	23. x	28. u	33. ff
4. o	9. a	14. c	19. bb	24. t	29. ii	34. z
5. f	10. p	15. b	20. cc	25. dd	30. v	35. w

Key Term Matching II

1. q	6. p	11. f	16. m	21. w	26. z	31. aa
2. h	7. b	12. g	17. e	22. hh	27. ee	32. gg
3. i	8. n	13. c	18. ii	23. r	28. u	33. t
4. j	9. o	14. d	19. bb	24. ff	29. v	34. dd
5. a	10. k	15. l	20. cc	25. s	30. y	35. x

Multiple-Choice Questions

1. C	6. D	11. B	16. B
2. B	7. D	12. D	17. B
3. C	8. B	13. A	18. A
4. A	9. C	14. D	19. C
5. C	10. A	15. C	20. A

CHAPTER 3
Biology and Behavior

You Should Know:

Nature and Nurture (*summary on pg. 100 of text*)

Introduction
- how the understanding of the role of nature and nurture has advanced to the present.

Genetic and Environmental Forces
- how the genotype of the parent, the phenotype of the parent, the genotype of the child, the phenotype of the child, and the child's environment are interrelated in a model of genetic and environmental influences on development.
- the process through which the parent's genotype influences the child's genotype, including an understanding of DNA and genetic transmission of genes, sex determination, and why children do not have the same genetic make-up as their parents.
- how the genes of an individual are related to the individual's phenotype, including what determines whether a particular gene is expressed or not and the mechanisms of Mendelian patterns of inheritance and polygenic inheritance.
- how the concepts of a norm of reaction and genotype-environment interactions relate to the association between a child's environment and the child's phenotype.
- how the active child theme comes into play in the association between the child's phenotype and the child's environment.

Box 3.1: Genetic Transmission of Diseases and Disorders
- the manners in which diseases and disorders are genetically transmitted.

Behavioral Genetics
- what the field of behavioral genetics attempts to decipher, as well as what behavioral geneticists presume about all behavioral traits.
- how behavioral geneticists examine the proportionate roles of environment and genetics and what premises underlie their research designs.
- how family studies of intelligence have shed light on the contributions of genetics and environment to intelligence.
- what heritability estimates do and do not tell us.
- the sources of shared and nonshared environmental effects and how they are assessed.

Box 3.2: Identical Twins Reared Apart

- what studies of identical twins reared apart have demonstrated about the heritability of many characteristics, as well as what the potential problems with these studies are.

Brain Development (*summary on pg. 112 of text*)

Structures of the Brain

- what the components of neurons are and what their functions are.
- what the cerebral cortex is, how it is structured, and the general functions of its lobes.
- what the cerebral hemispheres are, how they communicate, and how their modes of processing generally differ.

Developmental Processes

- how the developmental processes of neurogenesis, synaptogenesis, and synapse elimination work to structure the brain prenatally and throughout the lifespan.
- how nature and nurture influence these developmental processes.

Box 3.3: Mapping the Mind

- how researchers have employed various techniques to investigate which areas of the brain are associated with particular tasks.

The Importance of Experience

- the mechanism behind the influence of experience on synaptic preservation and elimination.
- why the brain produces an overabundance of synapses.
- how the brain is sculpted through experience-expectant processes, and how this type of plasticity leaves the brain vulnerable (<u>hint</u>: sensitive periods).
- how the brain is sculpted through experience-dependent processes.

Brain Damage and Recovery

- how plasticity and timing play roles in recovery from brain damage (i.e., when are the "best" and "worst" times to suffer brain damage?).

The Body: Physical Growth and Development (*summary on pg. 120 of text*)

Growth and Maturation

- the pattern of growth for humans and how growth patterns differ for males and females.
- how puberty changes the body and individuals' body image.
- how secular trends and environmental factors play a role in growth.

Nutritional Behavior
- the benefits of breastfeeding infants and why formula-feeding can support normal growth in some environments but not in others.
- the taste preferences that are present at birth and how experience and parental behavior are associated with taste preferences and eating behavior throughout childhood.
- the causes and consequences of obesity, bulimia, and anorexia nervosa.

Box 3.4: Eat Your Peas, Please
- what parents should and should not do to encourage healthy eating habits in their children.

Undernutrition
- how malnutrition and poverty interact to affect development and cognitive abilities, including both direct and indirect effects of malnutrition.

Key Term Matching I: Definitions

Instructions: Match each key term with its definition.

Set A

KEY TERM

1. _____	puberty	11. _____ heritability
2. _____	genotype	12. _____ heritable
3. _____	multifactorial	13. _____ lobes
4. _____	environment	14. _____ cerebral hemispheres
5. _____	phenotype	15. _____ corpus callosum
6. _____	alleles	16. _____ polygenic inheritance
7. _____	experience-expectant plasticity	17. _____ genes
8. _____	norm of reaction	18. _____ genome
9. _____	cerebral cortex	19. _____ menarche
10. _____	experience-dependent plasticity	

DEFINITION

a.   the two halves of the cortex

b.   the concept that refers to all of the possible phenotypes that could result from a particular genotype in relation to all possible environments

c.   the observable expression of the inherited genetic material, including physical and behavioral characteristics

d.   a dense band of nerve fibers that allows communication between the two cerebral hemispheres

e.   the basic units of heredity

f.   the onset of menstruation

g.   inheritance in which several different genes contribute to a particular trait

h.   the genetic material inherited by an individual

i.   traits or characteristics influenced by genetic factors

j.   the involvement of many factors, such as genetic and environmental factors, in an outcome

k.   the process by which neural connections are created and reorganized as a result of an individual's idiosyncratic experiences

l.   the gray matter of the brain

m.   a statistical estimate of the proportion of variability across individuals that is due to genetic differences among those individuals

n.   the complete set of genes possessed by an organism

o.   all aspects of the individual and his or her surroundings other than the genes themselves

p.   the process by which the normal wiring of the brain occurs as a result of the general experiences that every human in a reasonably normal environment will have

q.   major areas of the cortex

r.   the development of the ability to reproduce

s.   different forms of a gene for a particular trait

Set B

KEY TERM

20.	_____ axons	30.	_____ cell body
21.	_____ crossing over	31.	_____ myelin sheath
22.	_____ regulator genes	32.	_____ body image
23.	_____ anorexia nervosa	33.	_____ neurons
24.	_____ recessive allele	34.	_____ synaptogenesis
25.	_____ myelination	35.	_____ neurogenesis
26.	_____ glial cells	36.	_____ secular trends
27.	_____ dendrites	37.	_____ bulimia
28.	_____ mutation	38.	_____ dominant allele
29.	_____ synapses		

DEFINITION

t.   a change in a section of DNA

u.   the process by which neurons form connections with other neurons

v.   neural fibers that conduct electrical impulses away from the cell body toward connections with other cells

w.   the allele that, if present, gets expressed

x.   genes that control the activity of other genes, such as switching on and off

y.   cells that are specialized for sending and receiving electrical messages within the brain and between the brain and all parts of the body

z.   the part of the neuron that contains the biological material that keeps the cell functioning

aa.   discernible changes in physical development that have occurred over generations

bb.   how an individual perceives and feels about his or her physical appearance

cc.   the production of neurons through cell division

dd.   cells in the brain that provide supportive functions

ee.   an eating disorder that is characterized by eating binges as well as drastic efforts to avoid gaining weight

ff.   the junctions between the axons of one cell and the dendrites of another

gg.   the formation of the fatty insulation around some axons hh.   the process by which two members of a pair of chromosomes swap sections of DNA

ii.   the allele that is <u>not</u> expressed if a dominant allele is present

jj.   neural fibers that receive input from other cells and direct it toward the cell body

kk.   the fatty insulation around some axons that increases speed and efficiency of information transmission in the nervous system

ll.   an eating disorder that is characterized by starving oneself as a result of a distorted body image

Set C

KEY TERM

39.	_____	phenylketonuria	48.	_____ sex chromosomes
40.	_____	plasticity	49.	_____ frontal lobe
41.	_____	parietal lobe	50.	_____ failure-to-thrive
42.	_____	homozygous	51.	_____ cerebral lateralization
43.	_____	heterozygous	52.	_____ spines
44.	_____	chromosomes	53.	_____ DNA
45.	_____	behavioral genetics	54.	_____ association areas
46.	_____	marasmus	55.	_____ occipital lobe
47.	_____	temporal lobe	56.	_____ kwashiorkor

DEFINITION

mm.   long, threadlike molecules made up of two twisted strands of genetic material

nn.   molecules that carry the biochemical instructions involved in the formation and functioning of an organism

oo.   the chromosomes that determine an individual's gender

pp.   the lobe of the brain that is associated with memory and visual recognition, as well as the processing of emotional and auditory information

qq.   the phenomenon that each half of the brain is specialized for different modes of processing

rr.   a disorder related to a recessive gene that can cause severe mental retardation if the affected individual is not prevented from eating foods containing the amino acid phenylalanine

ss.   malnutrition brought about by the intake of inadequate protein

tt.   the lobe of the brain that is primarily involved in processing visual information

uu.   when a person has two of the same allele for a particular trait

vv.   the lobe of the brain that governs spatial processing and integration of sensory input with information stored in memory

ww.   formations on dendrites that increase the dendrites' capacity to form connections with other neurons

xx.   parts of the brain that lie between major sensory and motor areas and that process and integrate input from those areas

yy.   when a person has two different alleles for a particular trait

zz.   the lobe of the brain that is associated with organizing behavior and planning ahead

aaa.   the capacity of the brain to be affected by experience

bbb.   a condition in which infants become malnourished and do not grow for no obvious medical reason

ccc.   malnutrition brought about by the intake of too few calories

ddd.   the area of psychology concerned with how variation in behavior results from a combination of genetic and environmental factors

Key Term Matching II: Applications, Examples, and More

Instructions: Match each key term with an application or example of the term.

Set A

KEY TERM

1. _____ norm of reaction
2. _____ cerebral hemispheres
3. _____ failure-to-thrive
4. _____ environment
5. _____ cerebral lateralization
6. _____ dominant allele
7. _____ recessive allele
8. _____ polygenic inheritance
9. _____ experience-dependent plasticity

10. _____ behavioral genetics
11. _____ genome
12. _____ genotype
13. _____ genes
14. _____ phenotype
15. _____ cerebral cortex
16. _____ body image
17. _____ secular trends
18. _____ experience-expectant plasticity

APPLICATION OR EXAMPLE

a. mapping of the human _____ has demonstrated how much we have in common with other species

b. because the allele for brown hair is this, a child with brown hair must have at least one parent who has brown hair

c. this is a result of environmental factors acting in concert with genetic makeup

d. scientists in this field believe that <u>all</u> behavioral traits are heritable and that all develop within an environment

e. each of these codes for the production of a particular protein

f. most psychological and behavioral traits involve this, rather than Mendelian patterns

g. an example of this is the fact that American girls of today are experiencing menarche at an earlier age than did their ancestors

h. an individual's inheritance of two "brown hair" genes is considered to be part of this

i. this concept could be demonstrated by cloning an individual numerous times, placing the clones in a variety of environments, and observing differences in a trait such as intelligence or height

j.	identical twins differ in observable characteristics because of differences in this

k.	because the allele for blond hair is this, a child with blond hair may have parents who both have brown hair

l.	in general, these receive sensory information from and control the motor functions of the opposite side of the body

m.	an individual who generally appears to process information in a piecemeal, logical manner may be called "left-brained" by his friends because of this phenomenon

n.	this is considered to be the most human part of the brain, and it constitutes 80% of the human brain

o.	as a result of this type of plasticity, individuals are able to remember new faces and names

p.	this appears to be associated with disturbances in the mother-child interaction that occur as a result of characteristics of both the mother and the child

q.	as a result of this type of plasticity, individuals born with a lazy eye who do not receive treatment can become blind, as the affected eye is essentially disconnected from the brain

r.	American girls' _____ tends to be poorer than American boys'

Set B

KEY TERM

19. _____ alleles

20. _____ synaptogenesis

21. _____ sex chromosomes

22. _____ plasticity

23. _____ crossing over

24. _____ chromosomes

25. _____ homozygous

26. _____ glial cells

27. _____ phenylketonuria

28. _____ heritability

29. _____ neurons

30. _____ puberty

31. _____ heterozygous

32. _____ neurogenesis

33. _____ DNA

34. _____ mutation

35. _____ synapses

APPLICATION OR EXAMPLE

s.   humans have 23 pairs of these

t.   different sequences of this are associated with different traits

u.   dendrites and axons are components of these

v.   many inherited diseases and disorders originate from this mechanism for genetic diversity

w.   an individual who is _____ for a trait will definitely express this allele, whether it is dominant or recessive

x.   the gene for brown hair and the gene for blond hair are these

y.   as a result of this mechanism for genetic diversity, the chromosomes that parents pass on to their offspring are different from their own

z.   an individual who has one gene for blue eyes and one for brown eyes is considered this

aa.   this developmental process is essentially complete by approximately 18 weeks following conception

bb.   the strengthening of some synapses and the elimination of others that occurs as a result of experience is a demonstration of this brain capacity

cc.   a female has two of the same; a male has two different _____

dd.   neurons' electrical impulses are translated into chemical messages in these

ee.   these work to form a myelin sheath around some axons

ff.   the potential effect of this inherited disorder on affected individuals is a great example of a genotype-environmental interaction gg.   this developmental process begins prenatally and proceeds for some time after birth and results in a huge surplus of connections among neurons

hh.   estimates of this tell us nothing about the contribution of genetic factors to the characteristics of a particular individual

ii.   this developmental stage can lead to negative attitudes toward one's body, especially for girls

Multiple-Choice Questions

1. The genetic material an individual inherits is referred to as the individual's:
   A. genome.
   B. genotype.
   C. phenotype.
   D. environment.

2. Which of the following is <u>not</u> a mechanism for genetic differences between parents and offspring?
   A. dominant-recessive patterns
   B. crossing over
   C. mutation
   D. random assortment in the formation of germ cells
   E. All of the above are mechanisms for genetic differences between parents and offspring.

3. Traits that involve polygenic inheritance:
   A. are more likely to be expressed in males.
   B. are exhibited only when an individual is heterozygous for the trait.
   C. are produced from a combination of multiple genes.
   D. follow the Mendelian pattern of inheritance.

4. Disease Z is a dominant-gene disease. Individuals with which of the following genetic patterns will suffer from Disease Z?
   A. those with one Disease Z gene and one healthy gene
   B. those with two Disease Z genes
   C. those with two healthy genes
   D. A and B
   E. All of the above genetic patterns could produce Disease Z.

5. Lenny is a very active toddler who began to crawl, pull himself up to a standing position, walk, climb, and run at a very early age. Constantly chasing him and keeping him safe has made his parents very tired and stressed. As a result, they have gated off much of their home, only allowing Lenny to be in one nearly empty room (with a parent, of course) for a good part of the day. This is an example of the influence of a:
   A. child's genotype on his or her phenotype.
   B. child's environment on his or her phenotype.
   C. child's phenotype on his or her environment.
   D. parent's genotype on her child's genotype.

6. Behavioral geneticists believe that _____ of human beings' behavioral traits are influenced at least to some degree by environmental factors.
A. none
B. a small percentage
C. about half of
D. all

7. An adoption twin study is conducted to examine the role of genetics and environment on musical ability. Which of the following results would lead to a conclusion that environmental factors are <u>not</u> very important in determining an individual's musical ability?
A. Identical twins who were reared together are <u>more</u> similar in musical ability than identical twins who were reared apart.
B. Identical twins who were reared together are <u>no</u> more similar in musical ability than identical twins who were reared apart.
C. Fraternal twins reared apart are <u>more</u> similar in musical ability than identical twins reared apart.
D. none of the above

8. Findings that genetic factors have less influence on IQ before adolescence than during adulthood are indicative of which of the following?
A. genotype-phenotype association
B. genotype-parental genotype association
C. phenotype-environment association
D. parental genotype-environment association

9. Heritability estimates tell us nothing about:
A. relative contributions of genetic and environmental factors in the development of a trait in a particular individual.
B. the differences between groups on a particular trait.
C. the extent to which a trait is immutable.
D. all of the above

10. The degree of similarity between adoptive (genetically unrelated but reared together) siblings is attributed to their:
A. shared genetics.
B. nonshared genetics.
C. shared environment.
D. nonshared environment.

11. Which part of the neuron outputs information to other neurons?
    A. axon
    B. synapse
    C. dendrite
    D. cell body

12. Which lobe of the cerebral cortex is most important for spatial processing?
    A. temporal
    B. parietal
    C. frontal
    D. occipital

13. The two hemispheres of the brain are specialized for different modes of processing, a phenomenon referred to as:
    A. frontal lobe management.
    B. corpus callosum communication.
    C. cerebral lateralization.
    D. association area specialization.

14. Myelin serves as:
    A. insulation.
    B. connective tissue.
    C. path for communication.
    D. the cell body for some neurons.

15. The fact that babies with a "lazy eye," if it goes untreated, can become blind in the non-dominant eye demonstrates the:
    A. importance of experience in synaptic elimination and preservation.
    B. random nature of neuron creation.
    C. inability of infants and toddlers to coordinate the sensory information received from the eyes.
    D. fact that nature is more important than nurture when it comes to brain development.

16. During which of the following processes is brain damage <u>least</u> likely to lead to permanent deficiencies?
    A. neurogenesis
    B. neuron migration
    C. synaptogenesis
    D. Sustaining brain damage during any of the above are equally likely to lead to permanent deficiencies.

17. Which of the following is <u>not</u> a factor involved in nonorganic failure-to-thrive?
  A. infant's lack of interest in food
  B. mother's frustration at not being able to get her baby to eat
  C. infant's inability to stay awake to eat
  D. All of the above are factors.

18. Newborns prefer which of the following tastes?
  A. bland
  B. sweet
  C. spicy
  D. sour
  E. none of the above; Newborns have no taste preferences.

19. Individuals who starve themselves because of an extremely distorted body image are considered:
  A. anorexic.
  B. obese.
  C. bulimic.
  D. nervous.

20. Which of the following is an <u>indirect</u> effect of malnutrition?
  A. brain damage
  B. illness
  C. minimal exploration of the environment
  D. delayed physical growth

Essay Questions

Instructions: Answer the following essay questions on a separate sheet of paper.

1. Describe the concept of an X-linked disorder. Are males and females equally susceptible to these types of disorders? Why or why not?

2. Think about a trait or characteristic you possess that you are particularly proud to possess. Using the relations that are involved in the model of hereditary and environmental influence, discuss how you may have developed this trait or characteristic. Specifically, (1) How might your parents' genotype have directly influenced your genotype? (2) How might your parents' phenotype have influenced your environment? (3) How might your phenotype have evoked your parents' behavior toward you? and (4) How did you actively select your own environment?

3. Your friend reads an article about a twin study conducted to examine the heritability of mathematical intelligence. The article reports a heritability estimate of 55%. Your friend says, "See, this is why men are better at math and science than women." Is your friend's conclusion correct? Discuss why or why not.

4. Why do you think the text book singled out the cerebral cortex as the part of the brain on which to focus? What is special about the cortex?

5. Describe how synaptogenesis and synapse elimination work together in the development of the brain.

Answer Key

Key Term Matching I

1. r	9. l	17. e	25. gg	33. y	41. vv	49. zz
2. h	10. k	18. n	26. dd	34. u	42. uu	50. bbb
3. j	11. m	19. f	27. jj	35. cc	43. yy	51. qq
4. o	12. i	20. v	28. t	36. aa	44. mm	52. ww
5. c	13. q	21. hh	29. ff	37. ee	45. ddd	53. nn
6. s	14. a	22. x	30. z	38. w	46. ccc	54. xx
7. p	15. d	23. ll	31. kk	39. rr	47. pp	55. tt
8. b	16. g	24. ii	32. bb	40. aaa	48. oo	56. ss

Key Term Matching II

1. i	6. b	11. a	16. r	21. cc	26. ee	31. z
2. l	7. k	12. h	17. g	22. bb	27. ff	32. aa
3. p	8. f	13. e	18. q	23. y	28. hh	33. t
4. j	9. o	14. c	19. x	24. s	29. u	34. v
5. m	10. d	15. n	20. gg	25. w	30. ii	35. dd

Multiple-Choice Questions

1. B	6. D	11. A	16. C
2. A	7. B	12. B	17. D
3. C	8. C	13. C	18. B
4. D	9. D	14. A	19. A
5. C	10. C	15. A	20. C

CHAPTER 4
Theories of Cognitive Development

You Should Know:

Piaget's Theory (*summary on pg. 142 of text*)

View of Children's Nature
- Piaget's central assumptions about children and their learning.

Central Developmental Issues
- Piaget's view on the interaction of nature and nurture and on the continuities and discontinuities in cognitive development.
- the central properties of Piaget's stage theory.
- the general manners of thinking (as well as ages) of children in each stage.
- why children in each stage think differently.

The Sensorimotor Stage (Birth to 2 Years)
- how infants' thinking proceeds through six substages.
- how infants' intelligence is characterized within each substage, including their abilities and limitations of their thinking within each substage.

The Preoperational Stage (Ages 2 to 7)
- how young children's thinking is characterized, including their abilities and their limitations.
- how Piaget tested young children's thinking with specifically designed tasks, how children in this stage generally perform, and how Piaget interpreted their performance as an indication of cognitive limitations.

The Concrete Operations Stage (Ages 7 to 12)
- how older children's thinking is characterized, including their abilities and their limitations.
- how Piaget tested older children's thinking with specifically designed tasks and how children in this stage generally perform.

The Formal Operations Stage (Ages 12 and Beyond)

- how adolescents who have reached this stage are able to think, including cognitive abilities they did not have in the concrete operations stage.

- how the behavior of individuals in this stage differs from the behavior of children in the concrete operations stage when it comes to scientific experiments.

Box 4.1: Educational Applications of Piaget's Theory

- how Piaget's theory can inform educational practices.

- how Piaget's theory has been applied to teach children about the concept of speed.

Piaget's Legacy

- the strengths of Piaget's theory and how it has influenced current thinking about cognitive development.

- the most important weaknesses of Piaget's theory and how alternative theories are attempts to overcome these weaknesses.

Information-Processing Theories *(summary on pg. 154 of text)*

Introduction

- the characteristics common to information-processing theories.

- how cognitive development occurs according to this approach.

View of Children's Nature

- the general manner of children's thinking according to this approach.

- where this approach stands on the continuity-discontinuity and active-passive dimensions and why.

- how planning and analogical reasoning develop and influence problem solving at different ages and why young children sometimes fail to plan.

Central Developmental Issues

- how basic processes, strategies, and content knowledge change with development and how and why they influence the development of memory and learning ability.

- the difference between information that is encoded automatically and information that is not encoded automatically.

- how processing speed changes with age and why these changes occur.

Alternative Information-Processing Theories

- how connectionist theories, dynamic-systems theories, and overlapping waves theories build upon and differ from traditional information-processing theories.

- what types of problems each of the alternative theories has addressed successfully and how this has been done.

Box 4.2: Educational Applications of Information-Processing Theories
- how information-processing theories can inform educational practices.
- how analysis of children's errors can help them learn.

Core-Knowledge Theories *(summary on pg. 159 of text)*

Introduction
- the characteristics common to core-knowledge theories.

View of Children's Nature
- the general manner of children's thinking according to this approach.
- where this approach stands on its view of children's innate abilities and how this differs from Piaget's theory and information-processing theories.
- how research supports the existence of specialized learning mechanisms.

Central Developmental Issues
- the characteristics of children's innate understandings and in which domains these understandings occur.
- the characteristics of children's informal theories and why children form these theories in the domains in which they do.
- how research supports the existence of informal theories.

Box 4.3: Educational Applications of Core-Knowledge Theories
- how core-knowledge theories can inform educational practices.

Sociocultural Theories *(summary on pg. 164 of text)*

Introduction
- the focus of sociocultural theories' perspective on cognitive development.
- how sociocultural theories differ from the other theories in terms of the level of emphasis on the child as an active contributor to his or her own development.
- how children learn, as well as what factors influence learning and learning opportunities, according to this approach.

View of Children's Nature
- how Vygotsky's portrayal of children differs from that of Piaget.
- where this approach stands on the continuity-discontinuity dimension and why.
- how sociocultural theories view humans as unique among animals and as products of their culture.

Central Developmental Issues

- how cognitive change occurs, according to this approach.
- how communication plays a key role in learning and what characteristics of communication facilitate this role.
- how more competent individuals facilitate learning in less competent individuals and how this facilitation differs according to the competence of the less competent individual.

Key Term Matching I: Definitions

Instructions: Match each key term with its definition.

Set A

KEY TERM

1.	_____	connectionist theories	12.	_____ neural-network approach
2.	_____	selective attention	13.	_____ rehearsal
3.	_____	guided participation	14.	_____ adaptation
4.	_____	conservation concept	15.	_____ concrete operational stage
5.	_____	encoding	16.	_____ task analysis
6.	_____	overlapping-waves theories	17.	_____ formal operational stage
7.	_____	organization	18.	_____ sensorimotor stage
8.	_____	deferred imitation	19.	_____ dynamic-systems theories
9.	_____	preoperational stage	20.	_____ core-knowledge theories
10.	_____	intersubjectivity	21.	_____ symbolic representation
11.	_____	zone of proximal development		

DEFINITION

a.   the replication of another person's behavior a considerable amount of time after it has been observed

b.   the process of representing in memory information that is considered important

c.   Piaget's stage in which intelligence is developed and expressed through sensory and motor abilities

d.   an information-processing approach that emphasizes how variable children's thinking is

e.   Piaget's stage in which intelligence becomes logical, but not abstract

f.   a process by which more knowledgeable individuals organize situations to enable less knowledgeable individuals to learn

g.   the tendency to react to the demands of the environment in ways that meet one's goals

h.   the use of one object to signify another

i. the range of performance between what children can do unsupported and what they can do when they have the best possible support

j. the identification of goals, relevant information in the environment, and potential processing strategies

k. the tendency to integrate particular observations into coherent knowledge

l. the process of repeating information again and again in order to assist oneself in remembering it

m. the process of intentionally focusing on the information that is most relevant to the current goal while ignoring other information

n. a type of information-processing approach that emphasizes parallel processing

o. synonym for connectionist theories

p. an information-processing approach that emphasizes how various aspects of the individual function as a unified whole to produce behavior

q. Piaget's stage in which intelligence begins to develop through language and symbolic thought

r. approaches to cognitive development that focus on the sophistication of children's thinking in areas that have had evolutionary importance

s. Piaget's stage in which intelligence enables individuals to think abstractly and hypothetically

t. the mutual understanding that individuals share during communication

u. the knowledge that changes in the appearance of objects do not alter their fundamental properties

Set B

KEY TERM

22. _____ script

23. _____ centration

24. _____ joint attention

25. _____ accommodation

26. _____ equilibration

27. _____ sociocultural theories

28. _____ basic processes

29. _____ cultural tools

30. _____ social scaffolding

31. _____ problem solving

32. _____ personification

33. _____ A-Not-B error

34. _____ domain specific

35. _____ parallel processing

36. _____ assimilation

37. _____ social referencing

38. _____ utilization deficiency

39. _____ egocentrism

40. _____ sequential processing

41. _____ object permanence

DEFINITION

v. the tendency to focus solely on a single feature of an object or event

w. thinking that occurs one thought after another

x. the process by which assimilation and accommodation are balanced to create a stable understanding

y. a process by which more competent people provide a temporary framework that supports children's thinking at a more advanced level than they could manage on their own

z. the tendency to reach for objects where they have been found previously, rather than where they were most recently hidden

aa. the products of human ingenuity that enhance thinking

bb. the process by which individuals interpret incoming information into a form they can understand

cc. predicting the qualities of other animals from knowledge about humans

dd. the simplest and most frequently used mental activities

ee. the phenomenon that early uses of memory strategies are not as successful as later uses

ff. knowledge about how a type of everyday event usually occurs

gg. the process by which individuals adapt their current understandings in response to new information

hh. thinking that occurs simultaneously

ii.   limited to a particular topic

jj.   the process of using a strategy to overcome an obstacle and thus achieve a goal

kk.   approaches to cognitive development that emphasize the interpersonal context in which development occurs

ll.   the tendency to perceive the world solely from one's own view

mm.   a process in which individuals intentionally focus on the same external stimulus during communication

nn.   the tendency to look to others for guidance about how to respond to unfamiliar or threatening events

oo.   the knowledge that objects continue to exist even when they are out of view

Key Term Matching II: Applications, Examples, and More

Instructions: Match each key term with an application or example of the term.

Set A

KEY TERM

1. _____ conservation concept
2. _____ rehearsal
3. _____ sensorimotor stage
4. _____ task analysis
5. _____ selective attention
6. _____ guided participation
7. _____ concrete operational stage
8. _____ formal operational stage
9. _____ zone of proximal development

10. _____ preoperational stage
11. _____ deferred imitation
12. _____ dynamic-systems theories
13. _____ connectionist theories
14. _____ core-knowledge theories
15. _____ encoding
16. _____ intersubjectivity
17. _____ symbolic representation
18. _____ overlapping-waves theories

APPLICATION OR EXAMPLE

a.   social scaffolding allows children to perform at the high end of this

b.   individuals in this stage of Piaget's theory have object permanence but do not have a conservation concept

c.   research indicating that children simultaneously possess multiple arithmetic strategies, some more mature than others, lends support for this information-processing approach

d.   individuals in this stage of Piaget's theory can think deeply about concepts such as freedom and morality

e.   a father who shows his son to turn all of the puzzle pieces in the correct direction and suggests that his son put together the outside pieces first is engaging in this

f.   information-processing theorists attempt to understand and predict individuals' behavior with this

g.   researchers who take this approach have developed computer models that include large numbers of interconnected processing units

h.   a child who picks up a block, holds it to his ear, and says, "Hello?" is demonstrating his capacity for this

i.   this occurs automatically for some information, such as data on the relative frequency of events, but children fail to do this for other important information

j.   an individual who says a phone number repeatedly between the time she looks it up in the phone book and the time she dials the number is engaging in this

k.   a child who focuses solely on the spelling of words on her spelling list while ignoring the definitions of the words is engaging in this memory strategy

l.   a child who watches a line of closely-spaced pennies as they are spread out and believes that there are more pennies after they are spread out does not possess knowledge of this

m.   operating under this approach, researchers have demonstrated how the A-Not-B error is not simply an indication of incomplete conceptual understanding, but is associated with motor activities and attention as well

n.   individuals in this stage of Piaget's theory would be unlikely to give their daddy a pacifier if he gets hurt, but would still be unable to perform systematic scientific experiments

o.   theorists who support this approach believe that individuals are born with specialized learning abilities in domains such as identifying human faces and language learning

p.   a child who observes her father turn on the oven and then tries to turn the knob herself the following day is engaging in this

q.   this is unlikely without joint attention

r.   for much of the time individuals spend in this stage of Piaget's theory, they have no understanding that objects continue to exist when out of their view

Set B

KEY TERM

19.	_____	object permanence	29.	_____	assimilation
20.	_____	cultural tools	30.	_____	domain specific
21.	_____	script	31.	_____	basic processes
22.	_____	sociocultural theories	32.	_____	accommodation
23.	_____	problem solving	33.	_____	utilization deficiency
24.	_____	parallel processing	34.	_____	social referencing
25.	_____	A-Not-B error	35.	_____	centration
26.	_____	joint attention	36.	_____	personification
27.	_____	egocentrism	37.	_____	sequential processing
28.	_____	social scaffolding			

APPLICATION OR EXAMPLE

s. even infants have these mental abilities, but children are able to execute these more efficiently with age

t. an infant who realizes that a beach ball cannot be grabbed in the same way as her favorite rattle and thus grabs the ball with two hands has engaged in this process

u. a child who expects that his father will be home before dinner and then is surprised when he isn't has this type of knowledge about his family's evening routine

v. a child who searches for a ball that rolled behind a door, even though it has previously been found several times under the table, is <u>not</u> having this problem

w. core-knowledge theorists believe that learning mechanisms have this characteristic

x. examples of these are the symbol systems, artifacts, skills, and values that are part of the broad contexts in which interactions take place

y. key to information-processing theories is the assumption that children are actively engaged in this when they are trying to achieve goals

z. an infant who tries to grab a beach ball in the same way she has previously grabbed her favorite rattle has engaged in this process

aa. children whose early attempts to use rehearsal are unsuccessful are meeting this problem

bb. this concept requires the ability to mentally represent objects

cc. traditional information-processing approaches emphasize this type of thinking dd.   connectionist models rely on this type of thinking

ee.   Piaget used the three-mountains task to demonstrate this

ff.   by its very nature, this teaching behavior becomes less extensive as children learn to complete a particular task on their own

gg.   theorists who support this approach place less emphasis than do other theorists on the active role children play in their own development and a greater emphasis on the role of others

hh.   individuals must progress past this tendency in order to succeed at a conservation task

ii.   a mother who points to an airplane and says, "Look at the airplane," to her baby is counting on this in order for the baby to learn

jj.   a way in which children actively seek out the reactions of their social partners when faced with unfamiliar events

kk.   a child who believes that squirrels have tables and chairs at which to eat their acorns is demonstrating this practice

Multiple-Choice Questions

1. Which of the following is a true statement about Piaget's beliefs about learning?
   A. Children are intrinsically motivated to learn.
   B. Children need rewards and punishments from adults to learn.
   C. Children depend on instruction from adults to learn.
   D. Children's learning occurs purely as a function of biological maturation.

2. Six-month-old Hailey has been exclusively breast-fed since birth, and thus she never has drunk milk from a bottle. The first time Hailey is offered the bottle, she tries to suck on it the same way she is used to sucking. Hailey's sucking behavior is an indication that she has engaged in which of the following processes?
   A. equilibration
   B. calibration
   C. accommodation
   D. assimilation

3. Five-year-old children are generally considered to be in which of Piaget's stages?
   A. formal operations
   B. sensorimotor
   C. postoperational
   D. preoperational
   E. concrete operations

4. Mark and his mother are playing with an interesting rattle. Mark's mother is shaking the rattle in front of him and then hiding it under a large bowl. Mark is having fun finding the rattle under the bowl and then giving it back to his mother. After several rounds of this game, Mark's mother hides the rattle in a cabinet instead of under the bowl. Rather than looking in the cabinet, however, Mark lifts the bowl to look for the rattle. Mark is probably approximately what age?
   A. 1 month old
   B. 6 months old
   C. 12 months old
   D. 18 months old

5. Repetition of other people's behavior some time after it has been observed is referred to as:
   A. formal operations.
   B. post-observation modeling.
   C. symbolic representations.
   D. deferred imitation.

6. Which of the following is an example of egocentrism?
   A. Meredith picks up a block and pretends to talk into it like a phone.
   B. Jane gives her father a doll for his birthday.
   C. Matthew thinks 10 pennies are worth more than one quarter.
   D. Jing opens the cabinet to get a cup after seeing his father get a cup the previous day.

7. Raymond's mother pours a cup of milk for him and then realizes that the cup has a small crack in it. Not wanting her son to cut his lip, she pours the milk into another cup. The second cup happens to be shorter and wider than the first cup. Raymond starts crying because he thinks the second cup holds less milk than the first cup. Raymond is in which of Piaget's stags?
   A. formal operations
   B. sensorimotor
   C. postoperational
   D. preoperational
   E. concrete operations

8. Individuals in Piaget's formal operations stage suffer from:
   A. egocentrism.
   B. centration.
   C. lack of conservation concept.
   D. A and B
   E. all of the above
   F. none of the above

9. Task analysis is part of which of the following theories?
   A. Core-knowledge
   B. Information-processing
   C. Piagetian
   D. Sociocultural

10. Analogical reasoning involves which of the following?
    A. understanding new problems in terms of familiar ones
    B. planning a strategy to solve a problem
    C. testing several strategies to determine which will work
    D. completing a task analysis
    E. all of the above

11. Eight-year-old Jessica has a spelling test the next day. She has a spelling list, complete with the definition of each word and an example of the word in a sentence. When trying to learn the spellings of the words that will be tested, she does not focus on the spelling of the other words in the sample sentences. Jessica is using which of the following?
   A. analogical reasoning
   B. selective attention
   C. rehearsal
   D. utilization deficiency

12. Knowledge about how an everyday event usually happens is referred to as:
   A. rehearsal.
   B. recreation.
   C. a script.
   D. a plan.

13. The connectionist approach is also referred to as the:
   A. neural-network approach.
   B. dynamic-systems approach.
   C. core-knowledge approach.
   D. overlapping-waves approach.

14. Which of the following is a difference between Piaget's theory and core-knowledge theories?
   A. depiction of children as active versus passive learners
   B. view of the types of learning abilities that are innate
   C. focus on the importance of nature versus nurture
   D. expectation of the motivation involved in cognitive development

15. According to core-knowledge theories, informal theories of which of the following domains develop earliest?
   A. psychology
   B. biology
   C. physics
   D. Informal theories of all of the above domains are fully developed at birth.

16. Randy tells his mother that their cow is happy that they are drinking her milk. This is an example of:
   A. animification.
   B. objectification.
   C. emotionification.
   D. personification.

17. Which of the following is an example of guided participation?
   A. Jacob's father separates all of the large Lego pieces so Jacob will know he should start building the bridge with the large pieces.
   B. Emma's grandmother shows her how to bake cookies.
   C. Jose's teacher pairs Jose with another child who generally does not let him play in the group.
   D. Rhonda's uncle gives her explicit instruction on how to draw a house.

18. According to sociocultural theories, the processes that produce development _____ across cultures, and/but the content of what children learn _____ across cultures.
   A. are the same; is the same
   B. are the same; differs
   C. differ; is the same
   D. differ; differs

19. Joint attention is an example of:
   A. social scaffolding.
   B. guided participation.
   C. social referencing.
   D. intersubjectivity.

20. Which of the following constructs is <u>not</u> a part of sociocultural theories?
   A. intersubjectivity
   B. social scaffolding
   C. informal theories
   D. zone of proximal development

Essay Questions

Instructions: Answer the following essay questions on a separate sheet of paper.

1. Give an example of a conservation problem and describe how children in Piaget's preoperational stage, concrete operations stage, and formal operations stage would deal with the problem. What are the features of thinking in each stage that explain children's typical responses?

2. Describe three strengths and three weaknesses of Piaget's theory. For each strength and weakness, provide a specific example. In addition, for each weakness, state which alternative theory or theories (if any) discussed in the chapter addresses the weakness.

3. Describe how basic processes, strategies, and content knowledge work together to produce learning and improvements in memory. Give an example of a difference between what a young child and an older child would tend to remember after visiting a friend's house, and explain why these differences would occur.

4. Imagine you are a volunteer in the "Big Brother/Big Sister" Program, and you are helping your little "sibling" with his or her math homework. Describe the cultural tools involved in this interaction and how they influence the learning situation.

5. Describe the "jigsaw approach." What are the benefits of this approach, and why is it supported by sociocultural theories? Imagine you are an elementary school teacher, and you would like to use the jigsaw approach for the topic of weather. Provide a brief description of how you would use the approach.

Answer Key

Key Term Matching I

1. n	7. k	13. l	19. p	25. gg	31. jj	37. nn
2. m	8. a	14. g	20. r	26. x	32. cc	38. ee
3. f	9. q	15. e	21. h	27. kk	33. z	39. ll
4. u	10. t	16. j	22. ff	28. dd	34. ii	40. w
5. b	11. i	17. s	23. v	29. aa	35. hh	41. oo
6. d	12. o	18. c	24. mm	30. y	36. bb	

Key Term Matching II

1. l	7. n	13. g	19. bb	25. v	31. s	37. cc
2. j	8. d	14. o	20. x	26. ii	32. t	
3. r	9. a	15. i	21. u	27. ee	33. aa	
4. f	10. b	16. q	22. gg	28. ff	34. jj	
5. k	11. p	17. h	23. y	29. z	35. hh	
6. e	12. m	18. c	24. dd	30. w	36. kk	

Multiple-Choice Questions

1. A	6. B	11. B	16. D
2. D	7. D	12. C	17. A
3. D	8. F	13. A	18. B
4. C	9. B	14. B	19. D
5. D	10. A	15. C	20. C

CHAPTER 5
Infancy

You Should Know:

Perception (*summary on pg. 183 of text*)

Introduction
- the difference between sensation and perception.

Vision
- the methodologies used to examine infants' visual abilities and what they have demonstrated about infants' preferences and visual acuity.
- the general limitations of infant vision compared to the vision of adults.
- how infants' perception of patterns and objects develops, including how the cues used to perceive objects changes with development.
- how the cues used to perceive depth change with development and the methods used to study infants' use of these cues.

Box 5.1: Beauty and the Baby
- how infants' perception of the human face develops.
- what types of faces infants prefer and how these preferences have been studied.

Box 5.2: Picture Perception
- how infants perceive and understand pictures.

Auditory Perception
- how well infants' auditory system is developed at birth.
- how infants perceive aspects of music, what their preferences are, and how their musical perception is similar to that of adults.

Taste and Smell
- some of the tastes and smells preferred by infants and how these preferences are formed.

Touch
- how touch helps younger and older infants understand the world.

Intermodal Perception

- how intermodal perception has been examined in infants and what it has demonstrated about when their abilities develop.

Motor Development (*summary on pg. 192 of text*)

Reflexes

- what reflexes are, with examples of those that have adaptive significance and those that do not appear to have any adaptive significance.

Motor Milestones

- the general age range for the major motor milestones.
- how sociocultural factors can influence the timing of major motor milestones.

Current Views of Motor Development

- how current views of motor development differ from early views, and how the dynamic-systems perspective has broadened the view of what influences motor development.

Box 5.3: "The Case of the Disappearing Reflex"

- how systematic research conducted within a dynamic-systems approach has demonstrated that multiple factors are influencing the disappearance of the stepping reflex.

The Expanding World of the Infant

- how reaching and self-produced locomotion change infants' experience of the world.
- how infants' awareness of their bodies and motor abilities, as well as their perception of the environment, influence their reaching and locomotor behaviors.

Box 5.4: A Recent Secular Change in Motor Development

- how a secular change in motor development was apparently caused by a societal change.

Box 5.5: "Travel Broadens the Mind"

- how a long series of research studies has examined and demonstrated the interdependence of depth perception, fear responses, self-produced locomotion, and the social context of development.

Learning (*summary on pg. 199 of text*)

Habituation

- what the processes of habituation and dishabituation are and why they are adaptive.
- how the speed of habituation is associated with later cognitive ability.

Perceptual Learning
- what infants learn from paying attention to the objects and events they perceive.

Visual Expectancy
- how infants learn expectancies for future events and how this has been examined.
- how visual expectancy performance is associated with later IQ.

Classical Conditioning
- what classical conditioning is and what its component stimuli and responses are.
- how classical conditioning plays a role in everyday learning and emotional responses.

Instrumental Conditioning
- what instrumental conditioning is and what the limitations on learning in this fashion are.
- how learning through instrumental conditioning also teaches infants about their impact on their environment.

Observational Learning
- what observational learning is and how it develops with age.
- how children's understanding of intention plays a role in their observational learning.

Cognition (*summary on pg. 205 of text*)

Introduction
- how different theoretical perspectives point to different sources of infants' cognitive abilities.

Thinking About Things
- Piaget's perspective on infants' knowledge of objects and their permanence.
- how more recent research using two different methodologies has demonstrated more advanced knowledge of object permanence than the research concluded by Piaget.
- how the violation-of-expectancy paradigm has been used to examine a variety of expectations about objects by infants.
- how research has led to a number of explanations for infants' A-Not-B error.

Physical Knowledge
- how infants' physical knowledge, including an understanding of gravity, develops.
- how a series of studies using the violation-of-expectancy procedure has demonstrated infants' developing understanding of object-support relations.

Problem Solving
- what means-end problem solving is and when it develops.
- why this type of problem solving is difficult for infants.

Key Term Matching I: Definitions

Instructions: Match each key term with its definition.

Set A

KEY TERM

1. _____ unconditioned stimulus
2. _____ stepping reflex
3. _____ fovea
4. _____ conditioned response
5. _____ intermodal perception
6. _____ retina
7. _____ prereaching movements
8. _____ preferential-looking technique

9. _____ violation-of-expectancy
10. _____ self-locomotion
11. _____ unconditioned response
12. _____ conditioned stimulus
13. _____ auditory localization
14. _____ instrumental conditioning
15. _____ positive reinforcement
16. _____ classical conditioning

DEFINITION

a. a method for studying whether infants have a liking for one object or pattern over another that involves showing infants two patterns or two objects simultaneously

b. the back surface of the eye that contains the rods and cones responsible for translating light into messages sent to the brain

c. in classical conditioning, a neutral stimulus that comes to evoke the response by being repeatedly paired with the original stimulus

d. in classical conditioning, the response that was initially reflexive but comes to be elicited by the conditioned stimulus

e. a form of learning that involves associating one's own behavior with its consequences

f. a neonatal reflex in which infants move their legs in a coordinated pattern like walking

g. in classical conditioning, a reflexive response that is evoked by the unconditioned stimulus

h. in classical conditioning, a stimulus that evokes a reflexive response

i. a procedure used to study infant cognition that involves showing infants an event designed to evoke surprise or interest if it goes against something the infant knows or assumes to be true

j. a reward that consistently follows a particular behavior and increases the likelihood of the behavior being repeated

k. infants' clumsy swiping movements in the general vicinity of objects

l. the central region of the retina

m. the perception of the location of a sound source

n. the combining of information from two or more sensory systems

o. the ability to move oneself around in the environment

p. a form of learning that involves associating an initially neutral stimulus with a stimulus that always evokes a particular reflexive response

Set B

KEY TERM

17. _____ sensation	25. _____ stereopsis
18. _____ optical expansion	26. _____ pictorial cues
19. _____ binocular disparity	27. _____ contrast sensitivity
20. _____ reflexes	28. _____ perceptual constancy
21. _____ social referencing	29. _____ differentiation
22. _____ object segregation	30. _____ affordances
23. _____ perception	31. _____ visual acuity
24. _____ means-end problem solving	

DEFINITION

q.   the possibilities for action offered by objects and situations

r.   the depth cues that can be perceived by one eye alone

s.   the sharpness of visual discrimination

t.   the ability to detect differences in light and dark areas of a visual pattern

u.   innate, fixed patterns of action that occur in response to particular stimulation

v.   the difference in the retinal image of an object in each eye that results in slightly different signals being sent to the brain

w.   a depth cue in which an approaching object obscures more and more of the background

x.   the perception of the boundaries between objects in a visual display

y.   the pulling out of those elements that are stable from the constantly changing environment

z.   the processing of basic information from the external world by the eyes, ears, skin, tongue, etc., and the brain

aa.   the perception of objects as being stable in size, shape, etc., in spite of physical differences in the retinal size of the object

bb.   the use of another person's emotional reaction to interpret an ambiguous situation

cc.   the process by which the visual cortex combines the two images caused by binocular disparity

dd.   the process of organizing and interpreting sensory information

ee.   the process of performing an action to achieve a goal

Key Term Matching II: Applications, Examples, and More

Instructions: Match each key term with an application or example of the term.

Set A

KEY TERM

1. _____ stepping reflex

2. _____ auditory localization

3. _____ conditioned stimulus

4. _____ violation-of-expectancy

5. _____ self-locomotion

6. _____ instrumental conditioning

7. _____ preferential-looking technique

8. _____ unconditioned response

9. _____ intermodal perception

10. _____ conditioned response

11. _____ classical conditioning

12. _____ positive reinforcement

13. _____ unconditioned stimulus

APPLICATION OR EXAMPLE

a.   with this method, if infants look at one pattern for a longer duration than they look at another pattern, researchers conclude that infants can distinguish between the two patterns

b.   if her parents' clapping after she dances increases the likelihood that a toddler will dance in the future, the clapping is considered this

c.   in the example of the infant who has learned to cry at the mere sight of a doctor because of repeated pairings of the doctor and the pain of vaccinations, the crying as a result of seeing the doctor is termed this

d.   cortical maturation was ruled out as the cause of the disappearance of this by the examination of multiple factors such as leg weight and strength

e.   in the example of the infant who has learned to cry at the mere sight of a doctor because of repeated pairings of the doctor and the pain of vaccinations, the crying as a result of the injection is termed this

f.   with this procedure, infants are expected to look longer at an "impossible" event (such as, a screen appearing to rotate through a solid object) than at a "possible" event (such as, a screen that stops rotating at the location in which it would hit the solid object)

g.   in the example of the infant who has learned to cry at the mere sight of a doctor because of repeated pairings of the doctor and the pain of vaccinations, the injection is termed this

h.   Campos and his colleagues demonstrated that this plays a vital role in the development of fear of heights

i.   in the example of the infant who has learned to cry at the mere sight of a doctor because of repeated pairings of the doctor and the pain of vaccinations, the sight of the doctor is termed this

j.   infants' ability to pick out the video that is synchronized with the audio they are hearing is evidence of auditory-visual _____

k.   a toddler who now understands that others will clap when she dances has learned this through this type of learning

l.   newborns' ability to do this is demonstrated by their turning toward a sound

m.   an infant who begins to cry at the mere sight of a doctor has learned to associate the doctor with the pain of vaccinations as a result of this type of learning

Set B

KEY TERM

14. _____ binocular disparity
15. _____ differentiation
16. _____ visual acuity
17. _____ contrast sensitivity
18. _____ perceptual constancy
19. _____ pictorial cues

20. _____ sensation
21. _____ stereopsis
22. _____ object segregation
23. _____ reflexes
24. _____ perception
25. _____ means-end problem solving

APPLICATION OR EXAMPLE

n.   this is poor in infants, and thus only very different shades can be differentiated

o.   an example of this process is the experience of the taste and smell of peas evoked by the individual eating them

p.   some of these, such as rooting, have clear adaptive value, whereas others, like the tonic neck, have no known adaptive significance

q.   an example of this process is the activation of taste receptors on the tongue and receptors in the nose by the molecules in peas

r.   this process is infants' way of searching for order and regularity in the environment

s.   independent movement of objects is an important facet to infants' perception of this

t.   our brains use the degree of this as a depth cue -- the greater it is, the closer the object must be, and vice versa

u.   the maturation of the visual cortex is required for this; thus, binocular disparity cannot be used as a depth cue until infants are about four months of age

v.   these include relative size and interposition

w.   this can be assessed in infants by determining the smallest black and white stripes that they are able to distinguish from a gray square

x.   as a result of this phenomenon, infants perceive their mother as remaining stable in size despite the fact that their retinal image of her becomes larger as she walks toward them

y.   a young infant who does not realize he can pull the blanket his teddy bear is sitting on in order to get the out-of-reach bear is unable to use this type of problem solving

Multiple-Choice Questions

1. The habituation technique is based on the expectation that infants:
   A. look longer at objects they like or find interesting.
   B. look away from complicated or frightening objects.
   C. recognize patterns they have seen on previous occasions.
   D. lose interest in objects that are familiar.

2. A seven-month-old who is perceiving a subjective contour in a visual stimulus is:
   A. detecting a shape or object that can be seen by integrating only the overall pattern.
   B. perceiving differences in the sizes of circular objects.
   C. isolating the separate elements of a display.
   D. distinguishing between two-dimensional and three-dimensional objects.

3. Perceptual constancy enables us to do which of the following?
   A. recognize moving point-light displays as a person walking
   B. detect an illusory square from only four cut-out corners
   C. realize that the coffee cup in our current view is the same as the one we viewed prior to blinking
   D. perceive that the building across the street is very large although the image on our retina is small

4. For which of the following depth perception cues are both eyes necessary?
   A. pictorial cues
   B. binocular disparity
   C. relative size
   D. optical expansion

5. At what age are children able to localize sounds?
   A. at birth
   B. 6 months
   C. 12 months
   D. 18 months

6. An infant is placed in a crib that vibrates to a particular rhythm. At the same time, she views two television monitors on which a bunny jumps in two different rhythms, one that matches the vibration she is experiencing and one that does not match it. If she prefers to look at the monitor showing the bunny jumping to the matching rhythm, she has detected the similarity through which of the following?
    A. visual interaction
    B. proprioceptive perception
    C. intermodal perception
    D. inter-visual recognition

7. Newborn Seth feels something touch his left cheek, and he turns his head toward that side in response. Seth has just demonstrated which of the following reflexes?
    A. rooting
    B. tonic neck
    C. sucking
    D. grasping

8. The research by Thelen in which infants were immersed waist-deep in a tank of water was designed to examine which of the following?
    A. effect of weightlessness on reaching
    B. effect of weightlessness on posture control
    C. emergence of the swimming reflex
    D. disappearance of the stepping reflex

9. Campos and his colleagues demonstrated which of the following about non-crawlers' and experienced crawlers' heart rates when they were lowered over the deep side of the visual cliff?
    A. Non-crawlers show heart-rate acceleration.
    B. Non-crawlers show no change in heart rate.
    C. Experienced crawlers show heart-rate acceleration.
    D. Experienced crawlers show no change in heart rate.

10. An infant's sibling always jumps off his bed with a loud bang when he wakes up from his nap. He then comes downstairs and greets the infant with a tickle, making the infant laugh and cough reflexively. Eventually, the infant begins to laugh and cough reflexively when he hears the bang, even before he sees his brother. The infant has learned to expect his brother's arrival through which type of learning?
    A. visual expectancy
    B. classical conditioning
    C. observational learning
    D. instrumental conditioning

11. An infant is given a pacifier that causes music to be played from a nearby speaker whenever it is sucked in a particular pattern. At first, the infant's sucking pattern is random, but she eventually learns to suck with only that pattern in order to keep the music playing. The infant has learned this through which type of learning?
    A. classical conditioning
    B. visual expectancy
    C. observational learning
    D. instrumental conditioning

12. Parents who are concerned about their children watching violent acts on television are probably most concerned about which of the following?
    A. observational learning
    B. visual expectancy
    C. instrumental conditioning
    D. intermodal perception

13. Object permanence refers to the conception that:
    A. objects do not exist when one cannot act on them.
    B. one is unable to act on many objects because of their size or weight.
    C. objects exist independently of one's ability to perceive or act on them.
    D. none of the above

14. A six-month-old infant is struggling to reach a colorful rattle that is on the floor in front of her. The infant's mother mistakenly drops a blanket over the rattle, concealing it from the infant. Which of the following is the infant's most likely response?
    A. crying at her inability to reach the rattle
    B. laughing at the fact that she can no longer see the object
    C. reaching to uncover the rattle
    D. looking away from the covered rattle and instead picking up another nearby toy

15. Research examining infants' behavior when the room becomes dark after they are shown an attractive object demonstrated which of the following?
    A. Young infants are fearful of the dark.
    B. Young infants do not expect the object to still be there when the light is turned back on again.
    C. Young infants reach for the object even when they cannot see it.
    D. Young infants respond differently to possible and impossible events.

16. Which of the following techniques is based on the expectation that infants are surprised at events that are inconsistent with their knowledge?
    A. visual preference
    B. violation of expectancy
    C. habituation/dishabituation
    D. A-not-B error

17. In Baillargeon's research with short and tall rabbits moving behind a screen, infants were given which of the following hints about the true nature of the impossible event?
   A. The rabbits did not actually differ in height.
   B. The window in the screen was really a mirror.
   C. The short rabbit actually remained stationary.
   D. There were really two tall rabbits.

18. Which of the following makes it <u>more</u> likely that infants will make the A-not-B error?
   A. keeping the appearance of the locations distinct
   B. shortening the delay between A and B trials
   C. hiding the toy in location A on multiple trials
   D. allowing the infant to search immediately after the toy is hidden at B

19. Which of the following is the most advanced concept infants develop as they learn about support events?
   A. type of contact
   B. whether or not there is contact
   C. shape of supported object
   D. amount of contact

20. A six-month-old baby is struggling to reach a colorful rattle that is on a blanket in front of her. Although the rattle is out of the baby's reach, the blanket is well within her reach. Which of the following is the baby <u>least</u> likely to do?
   A. pull the blanket towards her in order to bring the toy closer
   B. try to move toward the toy
   C. struggle in vain to reach the object
   D. cry

Essay Questions

Instructions: Answer the following essay questions on a separate sheet of paper.

1. How do babies' object segregation abilities help them learn? Give examples to support your point.

2. Design a study to examine whether six-month-old infants favor happy faces to sad faces. Discuss the methodology you would use and what data you would need to conclude that they preferred happy faces.

3. Describe the role of visual perception in the development of reaching and self-locomotion.

4. Describe the following types of learning: classical conditioning, instrumental conditioning, and observational learning. Give an example of something a six-month-old infant might learn through each type.

5. The series of studies conducted by Baillargeon and her colleagues using the rotating screen has provided useful information about infants' ability to mentally represent objects and their characteristics. Describe these studies, including the methodology and the conclusions.

Answer Key

Key Term Matching I

1. h	6. b	11. g	16. p	21. bb	26. r	31. s
2. f	7. k	12. c	17. z	22. x	27. t	
3. l	8. a	13. m	18. w	23. dd	28. aa	
4. d	9. i	14. e	19. v	24. ee	29. y	
5. n	10. o	15. j	20. u	25. cc	30. q	

Key Term Matching II

1. d	5. h	9. j	13. g	17. n	21. u	25. y
2. l	6. k	10. c	14. t	18. x	22. s	
3. i	7. a	11. m	15. r	19. v	23. p	
4. f	8. e	12. b	16. w	20. q	24. o	

Multiple-Choice Questions

1. D	6. C	11. D	16. B
2. A	7. A	12. A	17. D
3. D	8. D	13. C	18. C
4. B	9. C	14. D	19. C
5. A	10. B	15. C	20. A

CHAPTER 6
Development of Language and Symbol Use

You Should Know:

Introduction

- what a symbol is and why the use of symbols is a crucial developmental task for humans.

Language Development (*summary on pg. 242 of text*)

Introduction
- which comes first, language comprehension or language production.

The Components of Language
- how children's language development involves multiple components: phonological, semantic, syntactic, pragmatic, and metalinguistic.

What is Required for Language?
- to what extent animals other than humans can be credited with language and communicative systems.
- how the human brain is specialized for language, as well as how language capacity is localized in particular areas of the brain.
- what the evidence is for the existence of a critical period for language acquisition and how this has implications for foreign language training and the education of deaf children.
- what the characteristics of infant-directed speech are and why this type of speech is beneficial for infants' language acquisition.

Box 6.1: Two Languages are Better than One
- what the developmental implications are of bilingualism.
- what the controversy in the United States is regarding bilingualism in the classroom.

The Process of Language Acquisition

- how infants and adults perceive speech sounds and how these perceptions are influenced by nature and nurture.
- what research has been conducted to examine infants' perception of speech sounds and what this research has demonstrated about the similarities and differences between infants and adults.
- what speech regularities are recognized by infants.
- what babbling is, how it develops, and how it and early communicative skills are influenced by nature and nurture.
- how infants' comprehension vocabulary and productive vocabulary develop at different rates and some of the difficulties infants encounter in each realm.
- the type of speech, types of words, and types of errors that are common in children's early speech.
- how adults influence children's word learning.
- how children actively contribute to their own word learning, including what types of assumptions they make about the meanings of words and what types of information they use to determine the meanings of words.
- how children's early sentences develop and what evidence exists for children's understanding of grammatical structure.
- how children's conversational skills develop and what parents do to influence the development of these skills.

Box 6.2: Variability in Language Development

- what language development styles have been identified and how children who adopt different styles ultimately fare in the successful acquisition of language.

Current Theoretical Issues in Language Development

- how nativists view language development and the cognitive abilities that support language.
- how researchers supporting an interactionist position view language development and the cognitive abilities that support language.
- how researchers supporting a connectionist position view language development and the cognitive abilities that support language.
- what support exists for each view, as well as what critics of each view argue.

Box 6.3: "I Just Can't Talk Without My Hands": What Gestures Tell Us About Language

- how gestures are associated with language development for hearing and deaf children.
- how deaf children who invented sign languages can inform researchers' views of the innate nature of language and its components.

Nonlinguistic Symbols and Development (*summary on pg. 247 of text*)

Box 6.4: Digital Development
- how computer use can benefit children.
- what concerns exist about children's increasing computer use.

Using Symbols as Information
- what is required in order for an individual to be able to use a symbolic artifact.
- how children's ability to achieve dual representation has been examined and what the research has demonstrated about the development of this ability.

Pretend Play
- how children's pretend play develops and what this type of play tells us about children's ability to use and create their own symbols.

Drawing
- how children's drawing ability develops and what this ability tells us about children's ability to use and create their own symbols.

Key Term Matching I: Definitions

Instructions: Match each key term with its definition.

Set A

KEY TERM

1. _____ language comprehension
2. _____ language production
3. _____ style
4. _____ phonological development
5. _____ collective monologues
6. _____ modularity hypothesis
7. _____ pragmatic development
8. _____ dual representation
9. _____ bilingualism
10. _____ categorical perception

11. _____ voice onset time
12. _____ object substitution
13. _____ holophrastic period
14. _____ generativity
15. _____ telegraphic speech
16. _____ semantic development
17. _____ narratives
18. _____ syntactic development
19. _____ metalinguistic knowledge
20. _____ intersubjectivity or joint attention

DEFINITION

a. the length of time between when air passes through the lips and when the vocal cords start vibrating

b. descriptions of past events that have the basic structure of a story

c. the notion that we can put together an infinite number of sentences to express an infinite number of ideas using the finite set of words in our vocabulary

d. the understanding of the properties and function of language

e. the learning of the system for expressing meaning in a language

f. the learning of the rules of how words can be combined in a language

g. the stage in which infants use one word at a time

h. the ability to use two languages

i. the learning of the sound system of a language

j.   children's first sentences that are generally two-word utterances

k.   understanding what others say or sign or write

l.   the sharing of a common focus of attention by two or more people

m.   the learning of knowledge about how language is used

n.   the strategies young children enlist in beginning to speak

o.   the perception of speech sounds as belonging to discrete categories

p.   young children's talk with one another that often involves a series of unrelated statements

q.   speaking (or signing or writing) to others

r.   the argument that the human brain contains an innate, self-contained language component separate from other aspects of cognitive functioning

s.   the notion that the use of a symbolic artifact requires mentally representing it both as a real object and as a symbol for something other than itself

t.   a form of pretense in which an object is used as something other than itself

Set B

KEY TERM

21. _____ symbols		31. _____ morphemes	
22. _____ pretend play		32. _____ infant-directed speech	
23. _____ expressive style		33. _____ overextension	
24. _____ syntax		34. _____ critical period	
25. _____ fast mapping		35. _____ prosody	
26. _____ wait-and-see style		36. _____ syntactic bootstrapping	
27. _____ pragmatic cues		37. _____ referential style	
28. _____ distributional properties		38. _____ universal grammar	
29. _____ reference		39. _____ phonemes	
30. _____ overregularization			

DEFINITION

u.   a set of highly abstract, unconscious rules that are common to all languages

v.   a speech strategy that analyzes the speech stream into individual phonetic units

w.   the smallest units of meaning in a language

x.   the phenomenon that, in any language, certain sounds are more likely to appear together than are others

y.   the time during which language develops readily and after which language development becomes more difficult and less successful

z.   a special mode of speech that adults adopt when talking to babies and very young children

aa.   the characteristic rhythm, tempo, intonational patterns, etc. with which a language is spoken

bb.   the rules of a language that specify how words from different categories can be combined

cc.   the strategy of using the grammatical structure of whole sentences to determine the meaning of novel words

dd.   the use of a given word in a broader context than is appropriate

ee.   a speech strategy that gives more attention to the overall sound of language than to its phonetic elements

ff.   a speech strategy that results in children beginning to talk at a comparatively late age

gg.   the elementary units of meaningful sound that produce languages

hh.   the process of learning a new word simply by noticing the contrastive use of it with a familiar word

ii.   speech errors in which children treat irregular forms of words as if they were regular

jj.   the association of words and meaning in language

kk.   aspects of the social context used for word learning

ll.   systems for representing thoughts, feelings and knowledge and communicating them to other people

mm.   make-believe activities in which children often create new symbolic relations

Key Term Matching II: Applications, Examples, and More

Instructions: Match each key term with an application or example of the term.

Set A

KEY TERM

1. _____ language comprehension
2. _____ holophrastic period
3. _____ dual representation
4. _____ pragmatic development
5. _____ metalinguistic knowledge
6. _____ collective monologues
7. _____ categorical perception
8. _____ voice onset time
9. _____ intersubjectivity or joint attention

10. _____ language production
11. _____ object substitution
12. _____ telegraphic speech
13. _____ bilingualism
14. _____ narratives
15. _____ modularity hypothesis
16. _____ generativity
17. _____ style

APPLICATION OR EXAMPLE

a. these sentences omit nonessential elements, such as word endings and function words

b. even though a child can understand his parents' words, it is not until she speaks her own words that she is considered to be demonstrating _____

c. with young infants, adults often establish this by talking about whatever the baby is looking at, but older infants are capable of following an adult's gaze

d. the learning of the cultural rule of referring to ships as female in the English language is considered part of this

e. this is supported by the fact that virtually all humans exposed to language successfully acquire it, whereas no other animals do

f. there appear to be cognitive benefits of this, and it does not appear to affect the course or rate of language development in either language

g. the finding that infants do this even for speech sounds they have never heard before demonstrates this is innate and is independent of experience

h. /b/ and /p/ differ only in this

i.   as a result of this, it is possible to form a sentence that that has never been uttered by any other person on earth

j.   a child who uses the word "nap-nap" to mean "I want to take a nap" is probably in this stage

k.   individual differences in this appear to have no long-term effects on children's ultimate language abilities

l.   a child who can understand his parents' words but cannot speak yet is demonstrating

_____

m.   this type of talk is common between preschoolers

n.   when children engage in this, they must ignore many of the real characteristics of the object so that it can serve the purpose of something else

o.   the understanding that all languages have words and that sentences are made up of words is part of this

p.   for a map, this involves both an understanding that it is a tangible piece of paper with lines and colors on it and an understanding that lines and colors on it represent roads, water, mountains, etc.

q.   five-year-olds' increased knowledge of the structure of stories helps them produce these

Set B

KEY TERM

18.	_____	wait-and-see style	28.	_____	syntax
19.	_____	phonemes	29.	_____	symbols
20.	_____	morphemes	30.	_____	universal grammar
21.	_____	expressive style	31.	_____	fast mapping
22.	_____	critical period	32.	_____	pragmatic cues
23.	_____	infant-directed speech	33.	_____	reference
24.	_____	prosody	34.	_____	overregularization
25.	_____	distributional properties	35.	_____	overextension
26.	_____	syntactic bootstrapping	36.	_____	referential style
27.	_____	pretend play			

APPLICATION OR EXAMPLE

r.   a child who uses the word "gooses" instead of "geese" is making this type of error

s.   newborns' preference for their mothers' language is due to their learning of this characteristic of the native language while in the womb

t.   a child who figures out the meaning of the novel word "basket" by her father's sentence "It's not in the bowl; it's in the basket" has used this

u.   even if one knew the meanings of all the words in the sentence "Big Bird gave Elmo the ball," one wouldn't be able to determine who was the giver and who was the receiver unless one understood the _____ of English

v.   the first utterances made by children with this style tend to be long "sentences" made up of hardly any recognizable words but uttered with perfect rhythm and intonation

w.   focus of attention and intentionality are examples of these

x.   in English, the word "cat" and the word "hat" differ in only one of these

y.   support for the existence of this comes from evidence that deaf children who had no linguistic input from adults spontaneously imposed a grammatical structure on their invented sign languages

z.   a child who thinks that the word "bird" represents the tall, leafy object that is inhabited by the small, black, singing object rather than representing the small, black, singing object itself, is having a problem with this

aa.   the first utterances made by children with this style tend to be isolated, monosyllabic words

bb.   case studies of children deprived of communication, along with studies of brain organization in individuals who learned a second language at different ages, have provided evidence for the existence of this

cc.   children with this style are apparently listening very carefully because once they do speak, they tend to begin with a large number of clearly articulated words

dd.   a child's use of the word "kitty" for the squirrels she sees outside, even though she can tell the difference between her own house pet and the animals with the fluffy tails, is an example of this

ee.   in English, the word "chair" contains only one of these

ff.   this involves high pitch and extreme changes in intonation and is generally accompanied by exaggerated facial expressions

gg.   children who heard the sentence "The duck is kraddling the rabbit" and understood that "kraddling" involved only what the duck was doing to the rabbit (and not what the duck and rabbit were both doing) used this strategy to determine the meaning of the new word

hh.   pictures, numbers, models, and maps are examples of these

ii.   infants are sensitive to this, as was demonstrated by the finding that they listened longer to rarely-combined sounds than to commonly-combined sounds after being "taught" a set of novel "words"

jj.   a child who uses a clean paint brush on the wall in a pretense of painting the wall is engaging in this

Multiple-Choice Questions

1. Learning which of the following is considered part of phonological development?
   A. how to produce the "r" sound
   B. the rules of negation
   C. how to take turns during conversations with others
   D. the contrast between the meanings of the words "table" and "desk"

2. Children's pragmatic development refers to their learning of the:
   A. meaning system and words of their language.
   B. cultural rules for how their language is used.
   C. rules for combining the words in their language.
   D. sound system of their language.

3. The critical period for language development applies to:
   A. learning of only the first language.
   B. learning of only languages that follow learning of the first language (i.e., second language, third language, etc.).
   C. learning of all languages, first and subsequent.
   D. There is no critical period for language development.

4. Which of the following is <u>not</u> a characteristic of infant-directed speech?
   A. extreme changes in intonation pattern
   B. extreme changes in volume
   C. slow and containing elongated pauses
   D. affectionate

5. Imagine a foreign language that contains two phonemes, /њ/ and /ξ/, which differ only in voice onset time (VOT). The VOT of /њ/ is much shorter (100 ms) than the VOT of /ξ/ (200 ms). Researchers are interested in how adult native speakers of this language perceive sounds that have all the same characteristics of /њ/ and /ξ/ except that they have a VOT that is <u>between</u> 100 and 200 ms. (Note that there are no phonemes in this language that fall between /њ/ and /ξ/.) Adult native speakers of the language listen to artificial speech sounds starting with a VOT of 100 ms and then with progressively longer VOTs until the sound /ξ/ is reached. How will these adults perceive the sound with a VOT of 130 ms?
   A. as a mixture of /њ/ and /ξ/
   B. as an unfamiliar phoneme
   C. as either /њ/ or /ξ/
   D. This sound will not be perceived as a speech sound.

6. Young infants perceive speech sounds:
   A. continuously.
   B. in their native language <u>categorically</u> and those not in their native language <u>continuously</u>.
   C. categorically, perceiving <u>fewer</u> phonemic contrasts than do adults.
   D. categorically, perceiving <u>as many</u> phonemic contrasts as do adults.
   E. categorically, perceiving <u>more</u> phonemic contrasts than do adults.

7. Research on infants' sensitivity to the distributional properties of the speech they hear demonstrated that infants:
   A. are able to recognize the syllables that are common in their native language.
   B. are sensitive to the recurrent patterns of syllables in their native language.
   C. cannot differentiate between all of the phonemes that sound different to adults.
   D. are aware of the prosody of their native language.

8. The association of a word with its meaning is referred to as:
   A. orientation.
   B. intersubjectivity.
   C. reference.
   D. prosody.

9. "Mine" is an example of:
   A. nouncentric speech.
   B. overextension.
   C. holophrastic speech.
   D. telegraphic speech.
   E. pragmatism.

10. Which of the following children exhibits what language researchers refer to as an expressive or holistic style of language acquisition?
   A. Isaac, whose utterances have good intonation patterns, but few recognizable words
   B. Ricky, who only speaks with isolated, monosyllabic utterances
   C. Brenda, who is nearly silent, but who understands much of her parents' speech
   D. Abigail, who comprehends few of her parents' utterances

11. The study by Brown in which preschool children were shown hands kneading material in a container demonstrated that young children interpret "a sib" to refer to:
   A. the material.
   B. the container.
   C. the act of kneading.
   D. any of the above

12. Which of the following is usually included in telegraphic speech?
   A. action verbs
   B. auxiliary verbs
   C. verb tenses
   D. none of the above

13. Marcus' "rule and memory" model of children's grammar states that children make overregulation errors when they:
   A. are unable to remember a grammatical rule.
   B. make up their own grammar rules.
   C. forget the correct form of an irregular word and thus use the general rule by default.
   D. cannot figure out the appropriate grammar rule for a particular context.

14. Which of the following statements made by a two-year-old is a parent most likely to correct?
   A. "Where the baby is?"
   B. "Me want no shoes."
   C. "No read book."
   D. "Sky green."

15. The term collective monologues is used to describe the common pattern of conversation among:
   A. infants.
   B. preschoolers.
   C. school-age children.
   D. adolescents.

16. Narratives primarily refer to descriptions of what type of events?
   A. present
   B. past
   C. future
   D. current

17. Which of the following views of language development supports the existence of universal grammar?
   A. nativist
   B. interactionist
   C. connectionist
   D. all of the above

18. Connectionist views of language development hold that the information needed to acquire language is:
   A. held in the brain's language module.
   B. learned in the social context in which language is used.
   C. universal to all languages.
   D. contained in the language itself.

19. To use a symbolic artifact, children must be able to represent the artifact as:
   A. a real object only.
   B. a symbol only.
   C. neither a real object nor a symbol.
   D. both a real object and a symbol.

20. To eliminate the need for dual representation, DeLoache and her colleagues used which of the following with two and one-half-year-olds?
   A. a scale model of a large room
   B. a map of a room
   C. a shrinking machine
   D. crayons and paper

Essay Questions

Instructions: Answer the following essay questions on a separate sheet of paper.

1. Imagine your new neighbors are recent immigrants from Brazil. They have an infant. Should your neighbors have any concern that hearing English will interfere with their baby's acquisition of their native language, including all of the sounds, rules, and meanings that differ from English?

2. Imagine a foreign language that contains two phonemes, /њ/ and /ε̌/, that differ only in voice onset time. The voice onset time of /њ/ is much shorter (100 ms) than the voice onset time of /ε̌/ (200 ms). Researchers are interested in how adult native speakers and infants from homes that speak this language perceive sounds that have all the same characteristics of /њ/ and /ε̌/ except that they have a voice onset time between 100 and 200 ms. (Note that there are no phonemes in this language that fall between /њ/ and /ε̌/, but other languages do use a phoneme, /ю/, with all of the same characteristics of /њ/ and /ε̌/, except that it has a voice onset time of 145 ms.) Adult native speakers of the language listen to artificial speech sounds starting with /њ/ and then with progressively longer voice onset times until the sound /ε̌/ is reached. How will native speakers of the language perceive the sounds with a voice onset time of between 100 and 200 ms? Why? How could infants' perceptions of the sounds with voice onset times of between 100 and 200 ms be examined? What is the likely result of this examination? Why?

3. Describe the characteristics of children's first words. Specifically, what types of words do children tend to say first? What types of words do they rarely say? Provide an example of each. In addition, what types of strategies do young children use to simplify words?

4. Choose an object that is important to you in some way (e.g., book, desk, hat) and discuss how you may have first learned this word as a young child. How might the adults around you have used this word when they were trying to teach you the word? What assumptions might you have made about what the novel word may have meant? What types of cues might have assisted you in learning the meaning of this word? Give specific examples to answer each question.

5. Discuss the concept of dual representation of a symbolic artifact and give an example of a symbolic artifact and its two possible representations. Why is the need to be able to represent a symbol in two ways necessary for the understanding of symbols?

Answer Key

Key Term Matching I

1. k	7. m	13. g	19. d	25. hh	31. w	37. v
2. q	8. s	14. c	20. l	26. ff	32. z	38. u
3. n	9. h	15. j	21. ll	27. kk	33. dd	39. gg
4. i	10. o	16. e	22. mm	28. x	34. y	
5. p	11. a	17. b	23. ee	29. jj	35. aa	
6. r	12. t	18. f	24. bb	30. ii	36. cc	

Key Term Matching II

1. l	7. g	13. f	19. x	25. ii	31. t
2. j	8. h	14. q	20. ee	26. gg	32. w
3. p	9. c	15. e	21. v	27. jj	33. z
4. d	10. b	16. i	22. bb	28. u	34. r
5. o	11. n	17. k	23. ff	29. hh	35. dd
6. m	12. a	18. cc	24. s	30. y	36. aa

Multiple-Choice Questions

1. A	6. E	11. B	16. B
2. B	7. B	12. A	17. A
3. C	8. C	13. C	18. D
4. B	9. C	14. D	19. D
5. C	10. A	15. B	20. C

CHAPTER 7
Conceptual Development

You Should Know:

Introduction

- what concepts are and why they are important.

- what factors are involved in conceptual development.

- how language development and conceptual development are related and how they influence one another.

Understanding Who or What (*summary on pg. 269 of text*)

Dividing Objects into Categories

- how children generally divide up things in the world and the form these categories take.

- what types of categories infants can form, how infants' category formation develops over the first year of life, and how this has been examined in research.

- how children's categorization improves beyond infancy and what contributes to this development.

Knowledge of Other People and Oneself

- what infants understand about other people and why this understanding emerges so early.

- when infants begin to develop an understanding of the self.

- what the role of play is in the development of the understanding of others, including Piaget's and Vygotsky's views about this issue.

- how children's understanding of others develops from ages two to five, including the components of children's theories of mind and the relations among the components.

- what errors preschoolers still make and how researchers have examined these errors.

- what controversy exists regarding how children acquire the ability to understand others.

Box 7.1: Imaginary Companions

- how children who have imaginary companions are similar to and different from those who do not have imaginary companions.

- what purposes imaginary companions serve for children.

Knowledge of Living Things

- what young children do and do not understand about living things.

- when and how children begin to differentiate between living and nonliving things and among different types of living things, namely humans, other animals, and plants.

- how children's beliefs about inheritance, growth, illness, and healing develop.

- what controversy exists regarding how children acquire biological knowledge, as well as what evidence researchers on different sides of the controversy use to support their positions.

Understanding Where, When, Why, and How Many *(summary on pg. 283 of text)*

Space

- how the brain is specialized for spatial thinking.

- how the ability to represent location relative to oneself develops in infancy, as well as what contributes to infants' sense of space independent of their own location.

- how the link between self-locomotion and spatial representation has been examined in infants and older children.

- how the ability to see influences spatial representation.

- how the abilities to represent location relative to multiple landmarks and relative to one's starting point develop.

- how the sociocultural context influences the development of spatial thinking.

Time

- how infants' and children's experience of time, including remembering the order of events and estimating the duration of events, develops.

- how children's ability to reason about longer time periods, in both the past and the future, develops.

- how children's ability to reason about time develops, including the constraints on this ability in younger children.

Causality

- how infants are able to reason about physical causation, including how these understandings have been examined.

- how infants' understanding of causality influences their memory and imitation.

- how toddlers' understanding of causality influences their problem solving.

- how preschoolers' beliefs about causality develop and how these beliefs influence children's reactions to magic tricks.

Number

- what young infants understand about number and how this understanding has been assessed.

- how infants' rudimentary ability to do arithmetic has been assessed, what these studies have demonstrated, and what controversy exists regarding the implications of this research.

- how children's understanding of number and arithmetic develops beyond infancy.

- how the ability to count develops, including what counting principles preschoolers appear to comprehend.

- how differences in language and sociocultural context influence the development of children's ability to count.

- how the understanding of the relative sizes of numbers develops from infancy into childhood.

Box 7.2: Magical Thinking and Fantasy

- how preschoolers' understanding about causality is related to their magical thinking and fantasies.

- what magical beliefs are common in preschoolers.

- how children develop beyond their magical thinking.

Key Term Matching I: Definitions

Instructions: Match each key term with its definition.

KEY TERM

1. _____ concepts

2. _____ category hierarchy

3. _____ perceptual categorization

4. _____ autism

5. _____ subordinate level

6. _____ basic level

7. _____ essentialism

8. _____ psychological constructs

9. _____ numerical equality

10. _____ theory of mind

11. _____ false-belief problems

12. _____ subitizing

13. _____ superordinate level

14. _____ theory-of-mind module

15. _____ personify

16. _____ naive psychology

17. _____ egocentric representation

18. _____ dead reckoning

19. _____ intention

20. _____ appearance-reality problems

DEFINITION

a.   tasks that test whether children understand that other people will act in accordance with their own beliefs, even when the child knows those beliefs to be wrong

b.   the ability to continuously keep track of one's location relative to the starting point and thus be able to return directly to it

c.   a hypothesized brain mechanism devoted to understanding other human beings

d.   the most general level within a category hierarchy

e.   a basic understanding of how the mind works and how it influences behavior

f.   the middle level within a category hierarchy

g.   a commonsense level of understanding of other people and oneself

h.   the belief that living things have an essence inside them that makes them what they are

i.   the desire to act in a certain way

j.   to attribute properties of human beings to other entities

k.   general ideas or understandings that can be used to group together objects, events, etc., that are similar in some way

l.   tasks that test whether children have a full understanding of divergences of appearance and reality

m.   a syndrome involving a number of intellectual and emotional difficulties, particularly in understanding and relating to other people

n.   the grouping together of objects with similar appearances

o.   the most specific level within a category hierarchy

p.   coding of spatial locations relative to one's own body, without regard to the surroundings

q.   ideas used to understand human behavior, such as desires, beliefs, and actions

r.   categories that are related by set-subset relations

s.   the realization that all sets of N objects have something in common

t.   a perceptual process by which adults and children can look at between one and three or four objects and almost immediately know how many objects are present

Key Term Matching II: Applications, Examples, and More

Instructions: Match each key term with an application or example of the term.

KEY TERM

1. _____   theory-of-mind module
2. _____   category hierarchy
3. _____   subordinate level
4. _____   superordinate level
5. _____   false-belief problems
6. _____   basic level
7. _____   naive psychology
8. _____   intention
9. _____   autism
10. _____   appearance-reality problems

11. _____   perceptual categorization
12. _____   theory of mind
13. _____   concepts
14. _____   dead reckoning
15. _____   subitizing
16. _____   egocentric representation
17. _____   personify
18. _____   numerical equality
19. _____   essentialism

APPLICATION OR EXAMPLE

a.   these help us make sense of the world by simplifying it and allowing us to use our prior experience to interpret new situations

b.   the study in which toddlers imitated what it appeared an experimenter was trying to do rather than what she actually did demonstrated that these children had a basic understanding of this

c.   this is a major component of infants' conceptual thinking, and often involves color or size

d.   although some animals who forage for food and then must return home possess this ability, people are not very good at it

e.   in the tool/screwdriver/flat-head screwdriver hierarchy, "flat-head screwdriver" is at this level

f.   when presented with a sponge that looks like a rock, a child who correctly answers that the object looks like a rock has demonstrated an understanding of these

g.   infants tend to use this to locate an object, even when their own position has changed

h.   the tool/screwdriver/flat-head screwdriver relation is an example of this

i.   Wellman suggested that preschoolers' _____ includes the knowledge that beliefs often originate in perceptions

j.   children fail these tasks when they do not fully understand that others can have different beliefs than they themselves possess

k.   objects within this hierarchy level generally have many consistent characteristics and thus this level is often the first one learned by children

l.   even young infants appear to have a sense of this

m.   researchers who believe that children have a specialized _____ point to brain maturation over the first five years and to autistic children's difficulties with understanding other people as evidence

n.   a child who says, "That truck wants to be up here, not down there" is exhibiting his tendency to do this

o.   preschoolers' belief that cows have a certain "cowness" that they inherit from their parents reflects this way of thinking

p.   even infants have a simple theory of this type, probably as a result of their intense interest in people

q.   in the tool/screwdriver/flat-head screwdriver hierarchy, "tool" is at this level

r.   children, and even teenagers, who are affected by this syndrome find tasks examining understanding of other people's minds very difficult

s.   some researchers believe that young infants are doing this to "solve" arithmetic problems involving one to three objects

Multiple-Choice Questions

1. Categories that are related by set-subset relations are considered to be members of a:
   A. perception.
   B. concept.
   C. hierarchy.
   D. superordinate.

2. Which of the following is an example of a category hierarchy?
   A. furniture/inanimate objects/table
   B. people/Daddy/Mommy
   C. plants/daisies/living things
   D. animals/mammals/cows
   E. vehicles/cars/trains

3. Infants generally categorize objects as belonging to the same category when they have:
   A. a superordinate-subordinate relationship.
   B. similar appearances.
   C. causal relations.
   D. cross-class correspondences.

4. Which of the following groups constitute members of the same perceptual category?
   A. cat, dog, tiger
   B. bat, fist, tennis racquet
   C. clothing, pants, necklace
   D. knife, fork, pitcher

5. Which level of the kitchenware/cup/coffee mug hierarchy do children generally learn first?
   A. kitchenware
   B. cup
   C. coffee mug
   D. They learn all of the parts of the hierarchy simultaneously.

6. Ideas used to understand human behavior are referred to as:
   A. beliefs.
   B. psychological constructs.
   C. perceptions.
   D. intentional constructs.

7. Which of the following is <u>not</u> a category in Wellman's model of preschoolers' theory of mind?
   A. basic emotions
   B. action
   C. reaction
   D. moral rules
   E. beliefs

8. Ellie, a four-year-old, is told a story about a boy who loves ice cream from the ice cream truck. One summer day, the boy stands outside on the street curb. When asked why the boy is standing there, Ellie will be most likely to answer which of the following?
   A. "The boy thinks the ice cream truck will come soon."
   B. "The boy wants ice cream."
   C. "The boy wants ice cream, and he thinks the ice cream truck will come soon."
   D. "He is waiting for his friend from across the street."
   E. "I don't know."

9. Marcy, a five-year-old, is shown a raisin box and then shown that it contains pennies. If asked what she had thought the box contained before being shown its true contents, Marcy will most likely say she had thought it contained:
   A. raisins.
   B. pennies.
   C. popcorn.
   D. quarters.

10. On false-belief problems, children who do not yet have a complete understanding of the relation between their own beliefs and others' beliefs:
   A. have difficulty understanding that other people could have false beliefs when they themselves know the truth.
   B. have difficulty understanding that other people could know the truth when they themselves have false beliefs.
   C. believe that others will not be convinced of the truth.
   D. believe that others will be difficult to fool.

11. The tendency to personify is common at what age?
   A. one year old
   B. five years old
   C. nine years old
   D. twelve years old

12. The finding that babies pay more attention to rabbits than they do to inanimate objects indicates that they:
   A. can distinguish between animals and inanimate objects.
   B. can differentiate between people and other animals.
   C. know that plants, animals, and humans all belong to the category of living things.
   D. all of the above

13. Which of the following do preschoolers generally believe are alive?
   A. people
   B. other animals
   C. plants
   D. A and B
   E. B and C
   F. A, B, & C

14. The view that living things have something inside them that makes them what they are is referred to as:
   A. spiritualism.
   B. soulism.
   C. essentialism.
   D. the life-force principle.

15. An infant's ability to retrieve a hidden object when remaining in a single location is evidence for the infant's representation of space relative to:
   A. her own body.
   B. the hidden object.
   C. the external environment.
   D. the starting point.

16. Which of the following is a true statement about five-year-old's ability to use landmarks to code the locations of hidden objects?
   A. They are <u>unable</u> to use landmarks to code the locations of hidden objects.
   B. They are able to use landmarks to code the locations of hidden objects when there is only a <u>single</u> landmark and it is <u>very close</u> to the hidden object.
   C. They are able to use landmarks when there are <u>many</u> possible landmarks but when one landmark is located <u>right next to</u> the hidden object.
   D. They are able to use landmarks <u>regardless</u> of the number of landmarks and proximity to the hidden object.

17. Older infants possess the ability to:
   A. estimate the timing of past events.
   B. estimate the timing of future events.
   C. detect the order of events.
   D. estimate the duration of events.
   E. all of the above

18. Manny, a seven-month-old infant, is watching his big sister jump up and down. His sister repeatedly jumps twice and then pauses to wait for Manny's giggles. As she jumps, Manny's sister says, "jump, jump." After a minute or so of this, Manny becomes bored and stops giggling. His sister then changes the pattern to one jump and "jump." Manny responds to this change with renewed interest and giggling. Which of the following statements is true?
   A. Manny dishabituated to the "jump, jump" pattern.
   B. Manny habituated to the new "jump" pattern.
   C. Manny has a rudimentary understanding of numerical equality.
   D. Manny cannot discriminate between the number one and the number two.
   E. A, B, & C

19. Subitizing relies on:
   A. counting.
   B. guessing.
   C. perception.
   D. addition.

20. When asked the question, "Which is more X or Y?", three-year-olds can typically answer the question correctly when X and Y are numbers between 1 and:
   A. 2.
   B. 5.
   C. 10.
   D. 100.

Essay Questions

Instructions: Answer the following essay questions on a separate sheet of paper.

1. How does infants' attention to perceptual similarities among objects help them learn categories? Discuss the implications of this for the notion of the active child.

2. Describe the importance of developing categories for children's understanding of concepts and causal relations.

3. How do three-year-olds typically do at false-belief and appearance-reality problems? How about five-year-olds? How could you try to teach a three-year-old to think more like a five-year-old about these problems?

4. Describe a typical preschooler's understanding of the differences and similarities among people, other animals, and plants.

5. Describe how the development of an understanding of time is continuous and how it is discontinuous.

Answer Key

Key Term Matching I

1. k	4. m	7. h	10. e	13. d	16. g	19. i
2. r	5. o	8. q	11. a	14. c	17. p	20. l
3. n	6. f	9. s	12. t	15. j	18. b	

Key Term Matching II

1. m	4. q	7. p	10. f	13. a	16. g	19. o
2. h	5. j	8. b	11. c	14. d	17. n	
3. e	6. k	9. r	12. i	15. s	18. l	

Multiple-Choice Questions

1. C	6. B	11. B	16. D
2. D	7. D	12. A	17. C
3. B	8. C	13. D	18. C
4. A	9. A	14. C	19. C
5. B	10. A	15. A	20. B

CHAPTER 8
Intelligence and Academic Achievement

You Should Know:

Introduction

- the historical background of intelligence testing.
- the implications of Binet's theory of intelligence for other aspects of psychology.

What Is Intelligence? (*summary on pg. 291 of text*)

Intelligence as a Single Trait
- what *g* is hypothesized to be and what evidence supports its existence.

Intelligence as a Few Basic Abilities
- what crystallized and fluid intelligence are hypothesized to be and what evidence exists to support their distinction.
- how Thurstone viewed intelligence and what evidence exists to support his view.

Intelligence as Multiple Processes
- how information-processing theorists conceive of intelligence.
- the benefits and costs of viewing intelligence as many things versus a few things versus one thing.

A Proposed Resolution
- how John Carroll proposed to resolve the different perspectives on intelligence.

Measuring Intelligence (*summary on pg. 295 of text*)

The Contents of Intelligence Tests
- how the content of intelligence tests varies with the age of the children being tested and why this is the case.
- what the most widely used intelligence test for children six years of age and older tests and how the sections are related to fluid and crystallized intelligence.

The Intelligence Quotient (IQ)

- what an individual's intelligence quotient tells us about his or her intelligence.
- the extent to which individuals' IQ scores are consistent over time and what influences the degree of consistency.
- what level of success researchers have had at measuring infants' intelligence.

Box 8.1: Gifted Children

- the two different types of gifted children and the common characteristics of the two types of gifted children.
- the factors involved in whether gifted children make outstanding contributions as adults.

IQ Scores as Predictors of Important Outcomes *(summary on pg. 296 of text)*

- how IQ is associated with long-term outcomes, as well as how other factors play a role.

Genes, Environment, and the Development of Intelligence *(summary on pg. 308 of text)*

Qualities of the Child

- the extent to which differences among individuals in IQ can be attributed to genetic differences, as well as how the genetic contribution to intelligence changes with development.
- how the three types of gene-environment effects proposed by Sandra Scarr contribute to individual differences in intelligence.
- how girls and boys are similar and different in intelligence and potential explanations for these differences.

Influence of the Immediate Environment

- how aspects of the family environment that may influence intelligence have been assessed and what association has been found between family environment and intelligence.
- how shared and nonshared family environments are associated with children's IQ.
- how school attendance is related to IQ, what types of evidence have pointed to this association, and the social policy implications of this finding.

Influence of Society
- how poverty is associated with IQ and what factors account for this association.
- what it means to be a resilient child and how resilient children differ from their peers.
- how race is associated with IQ, how these differences are influenced by differences in social-class background, and what facts we need to be aware of when drawing conclusions about these differences.
- what risk factors are associated with IQ scores and the implications of this research for demonstrating the importance of the environment in the development of intelligence.
- what interventions have attempted to improve children's IQs, as well as what factors influenced whether these interventions were successful.

Box 8.2: A Highly Successful Early Intervention: The Carolina Abecedarian Project
- the features of the Carolina Abecedarian Project, the extent to which the project was successful, and the implications of the project's success for the development of other intervention programs.

Alternative Perspectives on Intelligence *(summary on pg. 311 of text)*

- what Gardner and Sternberg believe is missing from traditional tests of intelligence and how they conceive of intelligence.
- what evidence exists to support the views of contemporary theorists and how we can reconcile these contemporary views with traditional conceptions of intelligence.

Acquisition of Academic Skills *(summary on pg. 325 of text)*

Reading
- how children's ability to read develops from birth through adolescence.
- how children develop phonemic awareness and how phonemic awareness in preschool is associated with later reading achievement.
- what strategies children use to identify written words and how they choose between strategies.
- what is involved in reading comprehension, how it develops, and what factors influence children's reading comprehension ability.

Box 8.3: Dyslexia
- what dyslexia is and what weakness accounts for most cases of dyslexia.
- what types of training can help children with dyslexia.

Writing
- what parallels exist between the development of reading and the development of writing.
- what skills are involved in writing and what types of strategies help children become better writers.

Box 8.4: Attention-Deficit Disorder

- what symptoms are associated with ADHD, and how ADHD affects the development of reading and writing.

- how nature and nurture play a role in ADHD and what treatments have been effective.

Mathematics

- what strategies children use to solve arithmetic problems, how children choose among these strategies, and how different types of children choose differently.

- how shallow understanding of mathematical concepts can lead to difficulty with novel problems, as well as what behaviors indicate that a child is ready to learn from instruction.

- how sociocultural factors influence children's mathematical abilities.

- what processes are important in learning algebra and how computer-based tutors can assist children with these processes.

Box 8.5: Mathematical Disabilities

- what difficulties children with mathematical disabilities encounter and what causes their difficulties.

- how interventions have attempted to help these children and the extent to which these programs have succeeded.

Key Term Matching I: Definitions

Instructions: Match each key term with its definition.

Set A

KEY TERM

1. _____ *g* (general intelligence)
2. _____ strategy-choice process
3. _____ fluid intelligence
4. _____ primary mental abilities
5. _____ ADHD
6. _____ phonemic awareness
7. _____ dyslexia

8. _____ visually based retrieval
9. _____ crystallized intelligence
10. _____ schemas
11. _____ phonological recoding
12. _____ IQ
13. _____ mental model

DEFINITION

a. proceeding directly from the visual form of the word to its meaning

b. processes used to represent a situation or sequence of events

c. strategies that can be applied to solving any problem within a class of situations

d. the inability to read well despite being of normal intelligence

e. a summary measure used to indicate an individual's intelligence relative to others of the same age

f. procedure for selecting among alternative ways of solving problems

g. the ability to translate letters into sounds and to blend sounds into words

h. the part of intelligence that is common to all intellectual tasks

i. the ability to identify component sounds within spoken words

j. factual knowledge about the world

k. seven abilities suggested by Thurstone to be crucial to intelligence

l. a syndrome that involves difficulty sustaining attention

m. ability to think on the spot to solve novel problems

Set B

KEY TERM

14. _____ three-stratum theory of intelligence		20. _____ gesture-speech mismatches	
15. _____ multiple intelligence theory		21. _____ phonological processing	
16. _____ normal distribution		22. _____ standard deviation	
17. _____ comprehension monitoring		23. _____ Project Rightstart	
18. _____ mathematical equality		24. _____ Carolina Abecedarian Project	
19. _____ Wechsler Intelligence Scale for Children		25. _____ theory of successful intelligence	

DEFINITION

n.   a curriculum designed to prepare kindergarteners from low-income backgrounds for elementary school mathematics

o.   a widely-used instrument designed to assess the intelligence of children ages six and older

p.   Sternberg's theory of intelligence that views intelligence as the ability to do well in life

q.   a pattern of data in which scores fall symmetrically around a mean value, with most scores falling close to the mean and few scores falling far from the mean

r.   a comprehensive and successful enrichment program for children from low-income families

s.   Gardner's theory of intelligence that claims that people possess eight intelligences

t.   a measure of the variability of scores within a distribution

u.   a phenomenon in which hand movements convey different ideas than verbal statements

v.   the process of keeping track of one's understanding of material as it is read

w.   Carroll's model of intelligence that proposes a hierarchy in which g is at the top and many specific processes are at the bottom

x.   the idea that the values on the two sides of an equal sign must balance

y.   the ability to discriminate and remember sounds within words

Key Term Matching II: Applications, Examples, and More

Instructions: Match each key term with an application or example of the term.

Set A

KEY TERM

1. _____ mental model

2. _____ phonemic awareness

3. _____ strategy-choice process

4. _____ schemas

5. _____ IQ

6. _____ crystallized intelligence

7. _____ phonological recoding

8. _____ visually based retrieval

9. _____ fluid intelligence

10. _____ *g* (general intelligence)

11. _____ dyslexia

12. _____ ADHD

13. _____ primary mental abilities

APPLICATION OR EXAMPLE

a.   high levels of this are associated with performance in school, with cognitive processing characteristics such as information-processing speed, and with high levels of knowledge of subjects not studied in school

b.   this process is used to read words without sounding them out

c.   children with this syndrome have particular difficulty with distractions

d.   these include reasoning, perceptual speed, and spatial visualization

e.   children with this syndrome read much less well than would be predicted by their IQ

f.   a child who has developed this understands that there are three distinct sounds in "bat"

g.   this tends to peak in early adulthood and slowly decline thereafter

h.   examples of this include knowledge of state capitals, past presidents of the U.S., and arithmetic facts

i.   a score of 100 on this measure indicates that an individual is of average intelligence for his or her age group

j.   reading comprehension involves forming a _____ of the situation or idea being depicted in the text and continuously updating it

k.   in reading, children use this to determine whether to sound out a word or retrieve it from memory

l.   a child who has developed this ability can sound out the written word "bat"

m.   the formation of these appears to a central process in learning algebra

Set B

KEY TERM

14. _____   three-stratum theory of intelligence

15. _____   Project Rightstart

16. _____   normal distribution

17. _____   phonological processing

18. _____   theory of successful intelligence

19. _____   gesture-speech mismatches

20. _____   Wechsler Intelligence Scale for Children

21. _____   standard deviation

22. _____   comprehension monitoring

23. _____   Carolina Abecedarian Project

24. _____   multiple intelligence theory

APPLICATION OR EXAMPLE

n.   a child who does not engage in this will not realize that he is not able to understand what is happening in a story he is reading and thus will not go back and reread a difficult passage

o.   this program attempts to give children from low-income families experiences common in middle-class families that teach mathematical lessons, such as playing board games

p.   this demonstrated the importance of beginning intervention programs early and continuing them for an extended period of time

q.   most children with dyslexia are poor at reading because of a general weakness at this

r.   this includes a Verbal section and a Performance section

s.   evidence of child prodigies who were exceptional in only one particular area and of brain damage patients who had only one particular deficit support Gardner's _____

t.   children who show these when they explain their incorrect answer are more likely to benefit from instruction than other children

u.   in a normal distribution, 68% of scores fall within one _____ of the mean

v.   this may resolve the controversy over whether intelligence is a single entity or multiple processes

w.   the fact that intelligence scores (along with many, many other variables such as height and weight) fall into this pattern allows for the assignment of IQ scores that are based on mean and standard deviation

x.   according to this, people who can build on their strengths, compensate for their weaknesses, and select environments in which they can succeed are considered of high intelligence

Multiple-Choice Questions

1. Positive correlations among dissimilar intellectual tasks has led to the hypothesis of the existence of:
    A. crystallized intelligence.
    B. general intelligence.
    C. fluid intelligence.
    D. three-stratum intelligence.

2. Fluid intelligence includes which of the following?
    A. knowledge of state birds
    B. ability to define words
    C. ability to draw inferences
    D. knowledge of grammatical rules
    E. all of the above

3. The three levels, from the top of the hierarchy to the bottom, as proposed by the three-stratum theory of intelligence are:
    A. "g", moderately general abilities, specific processes
    B. specific processes, "g", moderately general abilities
    C. "g", moderately general abilities, primary mental abilities
    D. primary mental abilities, moderately general abilities, specific processes

4. The Verbal Section of the WISC primarily measures:
    A. general intelligence.
    B. fluid intelligence.
    C. performance intelligence.
    D. crystallized intelligence.

5. IQ refers to:
    A. intelligence quarterly.
    B. individuality quotient.
    C. intelligence quotient.
    D. none of the above

6. The correlation between IQ at one age and IQ at another age is <u>lowest</u> for which of the following pairs of ages?
    A. 6 years and 7 years
    B. 6 years and 8 years
    C. 7 years and 8 years
    D. 7 years and 9 years
    E. A and C
    F. B and D

7. Which of the following is an example of a passive effect of the genotype on scientific understanding?
   A. Sally joins the science club at school.
   B. Gabriel loves the science museum, so his parents take him often.
   C. Charlotte is curious about scientific phenomenon, so her parents explain many to her.
   D. Blake's parents love to read about science, so they have many science books and magazines in their home.

8. Girls tend to be stronger than boys in:
   A. general intelligence.
   B. mathematical problem solving.
   C. verbal fluency.
   D. all of the above
   E. none of the above

9. Which type of variation seems to have the greatest impact on the development of intelligence?
   A. shared environment
   B. within-family differences
   C. between-family differences
   D. cultural characteristics

10. Which of the following is evidence for the conclusion that attending school increases IQ?
    A. Children's IQs increase with age.
    B. Children's IQs decrease over the summer vacation.
    C. Older children have slightly higher IQs than younger children in the same grade.
    D. all of the above

11. The gap between wealthy families and families living in poverty is greatest in which of the following countries?
    A. Canada
    B. Germany
    C. United States
    D. Great Britain

12. Which of the following is a risk factor on Sameroff's Environmental Risk Scale?
    A. African-American family
    B. maternal employment
    C. paternal education
    D. involvement of extended family

13. Project Head Start focuses on which facets of children's development?
   A. intellectual growth only
   B. physical growth only
   C. social and emotional growth only
   D. intellectual and physical growth only
   E. intellectual, physical, social, and emotional growth

14. Who is the founder of the theory of successful intelligence?
   A. Stanford
   B. Scarr
   C. Wechsler
   D. Sternberg

15. The ability to identify the component sounds within spoken words is referred to as:
   A. phonological recoding skills.
   B. strategy-choice process.
   C. mental model production.
   D. phonemic awareness.

16. The strategy-choice process involves choosing:
   A. among equally good strategies.
   B. the process that is least likely to result in an error.
   C. the strategy that will be fastest.
   D. the fastest approach that will be most likely to be correct.

17. Which of the following has the largest impact on reading comprehension?
   A. children's writing ability
   B. content knowledge
   C. strategy-choice process
   D. phonological awareness

18. Which of the following is <u>not</u> a contributor to the development of ADHD?
   A. sugar consumption
   B. genes
   C. prenatal exposure to alcohol
   D. abnormal prefrontal cortex activity

19. When asked what 3 + 3 equals, Chelsea immediately answers, "6." Chelsea has most likely used which of the following arithmetic strategies?
   A. decomposition
   B. retrieval
   C. counting from 1
   D. counting from the larger addend

20. Strategies that can be used to solve any problem within a particular class of situations are referred to as:

A. schemas.

B. representations.

C. values.

D. basic procedures.

Essay Questions

Instructions: Answer the following essay questions on a separate sheet of paper.

1. What do you think intelligence is? How should we define it? How should we test it?

2. Describe the three types of processes that Sandra Scarr has proposed to account for gene-environment relations. Give an example of each.

3. Describe the characteristics of the average early intervention project aimed at poor children's intellectual development. Were these interventions successful? In what ways were they unsuccessful? How is the Carolina Abecedarian Project different from these intervention programs? Do these differences matter in terms of the effects of this intervention?

4. Describe how traditional theories of intelligence differ from more recent alternative perspectives by Gardner and Sternberg. What are the advantages and disadvantages of the traditional theories? What are the advantages and disadvantages of the alternative theories?

5. What advice would you give to parents of preschoolers about what they can do to best prepare their children for becoming good readers?

Answer Key

Key Term Matching I

1. h	5. l	9. j	13. b	17. v	21. y	25. p
2. f	6. i	10. c	14. w	18. x	22. t	
3. m	7. d	11. g	15. s	19. o	23. n	
4. k	8. a	12. e	16. q	20. u	24. r	

Key Term Matching II

1. j	5. i	9. g	13. d	17. q	21. u
2. f	6. h	10. a	14. v	18. o	22. n
3. k	7. l	11. e	15. x	19. t	23. p
4. m	8. b	12. c	16. w	20. r	24. s

Multiple-Choice Questions

1. B	6. B	11. C	16. D
2. C	7. D	12. A	17. B
3. A	8. C	13. E	18. A
4. D	9. B	14. D	19. B
5. C	10. B	15. D	20. A

CHAPTER 9
Theories of Social Development

You Should Know:

Psychoanalytic Theories (*summary on pg. 337 of text*)

View of Children's Nature
- what factors Freud and Erikson viewed as driving development.

Central Developmental Issues
- where Freud's and Erikson's theories stand on the issues of continuity/discontinuity and nature/nurture and the extent to which they focus on individual differences.

Freud's Theory of Psychosexual Development
- what lasting contributions Freud's theory made on the field of developmental psychology.
- what Freud believed changed with development and how he conceived of each stage of development, including how the three personality structures develop during this time.
- how Freud believed healthy development culminated.

Erikson's Theory of Psychosocial Development
- what characterized each of the first five stages of Erikson's theory.
- what healthy development and unhealthy development look like at each stage and what parents can do to help children resolve each conflict successfully.
- how Freud's and Erikson's theories were similar and how they were different.

Current Perspectives
- how Freud's and Erikson's theories are viewed by contemporary developmentalists and why this is the case.

Learning Theories (*summary on pg. 342 of text*)

View of Children's Nature
- what learning theorists emphasize as important in the shaping of personality and social behavior.

Central Developmental Issues

- where learning theorists stand on the issue of continuity/discontinuity and the extent to which they focus on specific mechanisms of change.

Watson's Behaviorism

- how Watson viewed development, the role of the "mind," and the role of parents in development.
- how Watson's study of Little Albert has had a lasting impact on the treatment of fears and phobias.

Skinner's Operant Conditioning

- how Skinner's theory of operant conditioning has informed current thinking about child development and the ways that parents reinforce behavior unintentionally.
- how Skinner's theory led to the use of behavior modification.

Social Learning Theory

- how social learning theory is similar to and differs from traditional learning theories.
- the role of observational learning in development.

Box 9.1: Bandura and Bobo

- the types of questions and methods that typify social learning theory research.
- how Bandura examined the roles of observational learning and vicarious reinforcement in learning and what this research demonstrated.

Current Perspectives

- what lasting contributions learning theories made on the field of developmental psychology and what their major weakness was.

Theories of Social Cognition (*summary on pg. 345 of text*)

Introduction

- what role cognitive development plays in theories of social cognition.

View of Children's Nature

- what is viewed by social cognitive theorists as shaping development.

Central Developmental Issues

- what role the active child and individual differences themes play in theories of social cognition and where the theories stand on the continuity/discontinuity issue.

Selman's Stage Theory of Role Taking

- why role taking was considered by Selman to be important.
- how children's role taking ability progresses through four stages and how these stages are associated with stages of cognitive development.

Dodge's Information Processing Theory of Social Problem Solving

- what role cognitive processes are viewed to play in social behavior, according to information-processing theorists.
- what steps children proceed through when faced with a social problem and how children with a hostile attributional bias differ from other children in these processes.

Current Perspectives

- what lasting contributions social cognitive theories have made on the field of developmental psychology and what their major weakness is.

Ecological Theories of Development (*summary on pg. 350 of text*)

View of Children's Nature

- how ecological theories view children and the role of context and evolution in development.

Central Developmental Issues

- the extent to which ecological theories focus on the interaction of nature and nurture, the importance of the sociocultural context, and the role children play in their own development.

The Bioecological Model

- how Bronfenbrenner conceptualized the environment and the role of each environmental level on children's development.

Ethological and Evolutionary Theories

- what ethology is and how an ethological approach has been applied to developmental issues, including mother-child attachment.
- what the central premise of evolutionary psychology is and the types of issues on which evolutionary psychologists typically focus.

Current Perspectives

- what contributions these theories have made on the field of developmental psychology and what criticisms of these theories have been made.

Social Theories and Gender Development (*summary on pg. 364 of text*)

Introduction

- the extent to which research has documented similarities and differences between males and females.

Psychoanalytic Theory

- where Freud believed gender differences in attitudes and behavior originated.
- how gender differences in the development of the superego were believed to be influenced by differences in the conflicts experienced by girls and boys in the Phallic stage of development.

Social Learning Theory

- how girls and boys are hypothesized to learn different patterns of behaviors, beliefs, and values through observational learning and direct learning.
- what research exists to support the role of observational learning on gender differences.
- what parents and others may do to teach children gender roles and what research exists examining the extensiveness of parents' role in creating sex differences.

Box 9.2: Where Are Mrs. Rogers and Curious Jane?

- how television, books, and video games treat males and females differently and what research has examined the impact of this differential treatment on children's gender views and behavior.

Box 9.3: Asymmetries in Sex-Typing

- how parents and other adults perceive and treat children who exhibit behavior that is considered to be more appropriate for the opposite gender.
- what differences exist in the extent to which boys and girls are sex-typed and why this may be the case.

Social Cognitive Theories

- how Kohlberg proposed children come to understand gender and how they learn gender-appropriate behaviors.
- how gender schema theory addresses the problems of Kohlberg's theory.
- what gender schemas are, how they develop, and how they are expected to influence children's self-socialization of gender.

Ecological Theories

- how gender differences can be influenced by every level of developmental context and interactions among the levels.
- how evolutionary psychology and parental-investment theory explain gender differences.

An Integrative Theory: Maccoby's Account of Gender Segregation
(*summary on pg. 367 of text*)

- according to Maccoby, how gender segregation plays a role in gender development.
- the extent to which gender segregation exists in the U.S. and other cultures.
- what factors may contribute to gender differences in interaction styles and to gender segregation.

Key Term Matching I: Definitions

Instructions: Match each key term with its definition.

Set A

KEY TERM

1. _____ vicarious reinforcement
2. _____ erogenous zones
3. _____ systematic desensitization
4. _____ gender segregation
5. _____ superego
6. _____ internalization
7. _____ id
8. _____ Oedipus complex
9. _____ psychic energy

10. _____ reciprocal determinism
11. _____ self-socialization
12. _____ gender schema
13. _____ behavior modification
14. _____ Electra complex
15. _____ gender self-socialization
16. _____ ego
17. _____ imprinting

DEFINITION

a.   Bandura's concept that children are affected by aspects of their environment, but that they also influence their environment

b.   the notion that children actively shape their own development

c.   mental representations, including everything a person knows about gender

d.   in Freud's theory, the personality structure that is the rational, logical, problem-solving component of personality

e.   a process in which newborn birds and mammals of some species become attached to their mother at first sight and follow her everywhere

f.   in Freud's theory, the most primitive personality structure; it is unconscious and operates with the goal of seeking pleasure

g.   a form of therapy based on classical conditioning, in which positive responses are gradually conditioned to stimuli that initially elicit a highly negative response

h.   a form of therapy based on operant conditioning, in which reinforcement contingencies are changed to encourage more adaptive behavior

i.   observing another person receive a reward or punishment

j.   Freud's term for the biologically based instinctual drives that energize behavior, thoughts, and feelings

k.   in Freud's theory, areas of the body that are physically sensitive

l.   in Freud's theory, the personality structure that consists of internalized moral standards

m.   Freud's term for the psychosexual conflict experienced by boys, in which they have a form of sexual desire for their mothers and fear retaliation from their fathers

n.   children's tendency to seek out and interact with same-sex peers and to actively avoid opposite-sex peers

o.   the process of adopting one's parents rules and standards as one's own

p.   the process through which children's bias to behave in accord with their gender identity causes them to learn more about gender-consistent entities

q.   Freud's term for the psychosexual conflict experienced by girls, in which they have a erotic feelings toward their fathers and see their mothers as rivals

Set B

KEY TERM

18. _____ hostile attributional bias

19. _____ anal stage

20. _____ gender stability

21. _____ latency period

22. _____ genital stage

23. _____ role taking

24. _____ oral stage

25. _____ gender identity

26. _____ mesosystem

27. _____ parental-investment theory

28. _____ macrosystem

29. _____ chronosystem

30. _____ ethology

31. _____ exosystem

32. _____ microsystem

33. _____ phallic stage

34. _____ gender constancy

DEFINITION

r.   in bioecological theory, the larger cultural and social context within which all other systems are embedded

s.   the ability to adopt the perspective of another person

t.   the third stage of Freud's theory, in which sexual pleasure is focused on the genitalia

u.   the understanding that gender is invariant despite superficial changes in appearance

v.   the study of behavior within an evolutionary context

w.   the second stage of Freud's theory, in which the primary source of pleasure comes from defecation

x.   in Dodge's theory, the expectation that others' ambiguous behaviors originate from a hostile intent

y.   in bioecological theory, the immediate environment in which an individual directly participates

z.   in bioecological theory, historical circumstances that change over time and influence the other systems

aa.   in bioecological theory, the settings that influence a child's development but that a child does not directly experience

bb.   the first stage of Freud's theory, in which the primary source of gratification is sucking and eating

cc.   in bioecological theory, the interconnections among aspects of the immediate environment

dd.   the fifth and final stage of Freud's theory, in which sexual maturation is complete and sexual intercourse becomes a major goal

ee.   a theory that stresses the evolutionary basis of parental behavior, including the enormous amounts of time, energy, and resources parents devote to their children

ff.   awareness of one's gender

gg.   awareness that gender is stable over time

hh.   the fourth stage of Freud's theory, in which sexual energy gets channeled into socially acceptable activities

Key Term Matching II: Applications, Examples, and More

Instructions: Match each key term with an application or example of the term.

Set A

KEY TERM

1. _____ psychic energy
2. _____ Electra complex
3. _____ id
4. _____ vicarious reinforcement
5. _____ imprinting
6. _____ gender self-socialization
7. _____ erogenous zones
8. _____ behavior modification
9. _____ gender schema

10. _____ Oedipus complex
11. _____ self-socialization
12. _____ superego
13. _____ reciprocal determinism
14. _____ systematic desensitization
15. _____ ego
16. _____ gender segregation
17. _____ internalization

APPLICATION OR EXAMPLE

a. according to social cognitive theories, this involves children's adoption of particular goals to guide their own behavior based on their knowledge and beliefs about themselves and others

b. according to Freud, psychic energy becomes focused in these during various stages of development

c. this type of therapy is particularly useful for changing undesirable behaviors

d. this personality structure is ruled by the reality principle

e. the personality structure that is generally thought of as the conscience

f. Maccoby proposed that this stems mostly from the different interaction styles of boys and girls

g. this type of therapy is particularly useful in the treatment of fears and phobias

h. Freud believed that this conflict was not as strong for girls as boys' conflict was for them, and thus that girls do not develop as strong a superego as do boys

i.   Bandura's "Bobo doll" study demonstrated the effectiveness of this for increasing and decreasing the likelihood that children will imitate a behavior

j.   Bandura's concept of this demonstrates his view that children play an active role in their own development

k.   according to Freud, this is initially focused on bodily needs but some of it becomes diverted and transformed into psychological needs and desires in later stages of development

l.   this ensures that the baby will stay near a source of protection and food

m.   Freud believed that, to cope with this, boys increase their identification with their fathers and thus develop a strong superego

n.   this includes children's memories of interactions with males and females and gender stereotypes transmitted by adults, peers, and the media

o.   this personality structure is most apparent in selfish behavior in which immediate gratification is sought with little or no regard for consequences

p.   this process accounts for young girls acquiring greater knowledge about dolls and kitchen sets than about trucks and construction sets

q.   this process allows for the formation of the superego

Set B

KEY TERM

18. _____ latency period
19. _____ anal stage
20. _____ mesosystem
21. _____ oral stage
22. _____ genital stage
23. _____ ethology
24. _____ gender identity
25. _____ microsystem
26. _____ phallic stage

27. _____ exosystem
28. _____ macrosystem
29. _____ chronosystem
30. _____ role taking
31. _____ parental-investment theory
32. _____ hostile attributional bias
33. _____ gender constancy
34. _____ gender stability

APPLICATION OR EXAMPLE

r.   during much of this stage of Freud's theory, the only personality structure ruling the individual is the id

s.   this level of the developmental context includes a child's family and school

t.   this level of the developmental context includes the subcultural groups to which a child belongs as well as the laws and values of society

u.   during this stage of Freud's theory, sexual desires are safely hidden away in the unconscious

v.   this attempts to explain the relatively increased violence of stepparents toward stepchildren in terms of the fact that stepchildren cannot perpetuate one's genes are thus are less worthy of time, energy, and resources

w.   Selman believed this was crucial to the understanding of others' motives, thoughts, and feelings

x.   this can become a self-fulfilling prophecy, as children who possess it respond aggressively to peers, eliciting counterattacks and rejection by peers, further supporting the child's belief in others' antagonism

y.   children who are in this stage of Kohlberg's cognitive developmental theory realize that if they are a girl, they will always be a girl, but they do not yet realize that gender is independent of appearance

z.   this level of the developmental context includes parents' interactions with a child's peers

aa.   this level of the developmental context includes the age of the child when exposed to particular events bb.   according to Freud, this stage spans the ages of 3 to 6

cc.   this level of the developmental context includes the school board and parents' workplaces

dd.   this involves attempting to understand behavior in terms of its adaptive value; for example applying the concept of imprinting to the process of human infant attachment

ee.   this stage of Freud's theory begins in adolescence

ff.   according to Kohlberg's cognitive developmental theory, this is the earliest stage of gender development, in which children do not yet understand that their gender is permanent

gg.   during this stage of Freud's theory, conflict arises when parents begin to make demands on the child regarding toilet training

hh.   according to Kohlberg's cognitive developmental theory, this is the final stage of gender development, in which children understand that gender is consistent across situations and that if a boy puts on a dress, he is still a boy

Multiple-Choice Questions

1. Freud's theory is generally referred to as a theory of:
   A. psychosocial development.
   B. psychosexual development.
   C. social learning.
   D. social problem solving.

2. According to Freud, psychic energy is primarily focused on:
   A. erogenous zones.
   B. the ego.
   C. development of identity.
   D. the conscience.

3. The ego is ruled by:
   A. the conscience.
   B. the pleasure principle.
   C. conscious impulses.
   D. the reality principle.

4. According to Erikson, children who doubt their abilities or feel a general sense of shame have not resolved which of the following conflicts successfully?
   A. Autonomy vs. Shame and Doubt
   B. Initiative vs. Guilt
   C. Industry vs. Inferiority
   D. Identity vs. Role Confusion

5. Traditional learning theorists considered children to be _____ in their own development. Recent social learning theorists place an emphasis on children as _____ in their own development.
   A. active; active
   B. active; passive
   C. passive; active
   D. passive; passive

6. Each time two-year-old Janice hits her brother, her parents give her a "time out" with the expectation that this will cause Janice to stop hitting. This strategy is based on the principles of:
   A. operant conditioning.
   B. classical conditioning.
   C. social learning.
   D. systematic desensitization.

7. Albert Bandura's "social cognitive theory" differed from other learning theories in that it proposed that:
   A. development is discontinuous.
   B. reinforcement has no part in development.
   C. children play an active role in their own development.
   D. punishment is more important than positive reinforcement.

8. Aggressive children's hostile attributional bias occurs during which step(s) of Dodge's information-processing?
   A. enacting a behavior
   B. formulating a goal
   C. encoding an event and interpreting social cues
   D. generating strategies and evaluating likely success of strategies

9. Which of the following lists the levels of environmental influences from closest to the child to farthest from the child?
   A. microsystem, exosystem, macrosystem
   B. macrosystem, microsystem, exosystem
   C. exosystem, microsystem, macrosystem
   D. microsystem, macrosystem, exosystem

10. The microsystem involves the:
    A. settings in which the child is not a direct participant.
    B. general beliefs, values, customs, and laws of the larger society.
    C. activities, roles, and relationships in which the child directly participates.
    D. connections among the contexts in which the child directly participates.

11. The prolonged period of human children's immaturity is most interesting to which theorists?
    A. bioecological
    B. information-processing
    C. evolutionary
    D. behaviorist

12. According to Freud, gender differences originate from:
    A. gender segregation.
    B. children's identification with the same-sex parent.
    C. genetic differences.
    D. observations of same- and opposite-sex models.

13. Successful resolution of the Oedipus Complex involves:
   A. marriage.
   B. penis envy.
   C. sexual repression.
   D. the development of a conscience.

14. According to social learning theory, Cheryl, a four-year-old girl, would be least likely to learn by watching the behavior of which of the following people?
   A. Julia, her mother
   B. Matthew, a neighbor boy
   C. Mrs. Delaney, her preschool teacher
   D. Jillian, a girl in her class

15. Which of the following reflects parental reinforcement of gender-appropriate behavior?
   A. Infants show preferences for toys considered gender-appropriate.
   B. Parents are more responsive to children when they are engaging in sex-appropriate play than when they are engaging in cross-sex play.
   C. Children pay more attention to same-sex models than to opposite-sex models.
   D. all of the above

16. Which of the following lists Kohlberg's stages of the development of gender knowledge in the correct chronological order, from earliest to latest?
   A. gender stability, gender identity, gender constancy
   B. gender identity, gender constancy, gender stability
   C. gender constancy, gender identity, gender stability
   D. gender identity, gender stability, gender constancy

17. Kohlberg's concept of gender identity involves the understanding that:
   A. one is a member of one gender category or another.
   B. gender is consistent even when superficial changes occur.
   C. gender is stable over time.
   D. gender is determined by sex chromosomes.

18. Which of the following is not an effect of gender schemas?
   A. biased processing of information about gender
   B. biased recall of gender information
   C. perpetuation of incorrect gender stereotypes
   D. All of the above are effects of gender schemas.

19. Which of the following is a gender difference in children's mesosystem?
  A. Girls' and boys' rooms are often decorated quite differently.
  B. Males tend to be valued in society more highly than girls.
  C. Parents expect girls to be better at language and boys to be better at math.
  D. The occupational roles that are available for men and women differ.

20. Evolutionary psychologists would be most interested in which of the following?
  A. gender differences in aggression
  B. societal values and customs
  C. differences in the ways parents structure boys' and girls' living spaces
  D. children's realization of the differences between individuals who have a penis and those who do not

Essay Questions

Instructions: Answer the following essay questions on a separate sheet of paper.

1. Think about a difficult decision you have recently made or a conflict you have recently experienced – with a sibling, parent, roommate, friend, significant other, or professor. Describe the situation and the role each of your three personality structures played in this situation. In other words, according to Freud, what were the goals of your id, your ego, and your superego, and how did these goals influence the final decision or conflict resolution?

2. Describe Bandura's view of observational learning. Be sure your description includes answers to the following two questions: (1) Do children need reinforcement to be able to learn from imitation? (2) What cognitive processes are involved in such learning?

3. From the perspective of the bioecological model, describe the contexts in which you are currently developing. How are the relationships among the microsystems bi-directional? Also, how do you actively influence these contexts?

4. Although a great deal of research has been directed toward exposing the differences between the ways parents treat their sons and daughters, few differences have been found. Discuss at least two ways that parents' treatment of their boys and girls is similar and at least two ways that it has been found to be different.

5. Describe Maccoby's theory of the development of gender differences. Be specific and give supportive examples.

Answer Key

Key Term Matching I

1. i	6. o	11. b	16. d	21. hh	26. cc	31. aa
2. k	7. f	12. c	17. e	22. dd	27. ee	32. y
3. g	8. m	13. h	18. x	23. s	28. r	33. t
4. n	9. j	14. q	19. w	24. bb	29. z	34. u
5. l	10. a	15. p	20. gg	25. ff	30. v	

Key Term Matching II

1. k	6. p	11. a	16. f	21. r	26. bb	31. v
2. h	7. b	12. e	17. q	22. ee	27. cc	32. x
3. o	8. c	13. j	18. u	23. dd	28. t	33. hh
4. i	9. n	14. g	19. gg	24. ff	29. aa	34. y
5. l	10. m	15. d	20. z	25. s	30. w	

Multiple-Choice Questions

1. B	6. A	11. C	16. D
2. A	7. C	12. B	17. A
3. D	8. C	13. D	18. D
4. A	9. A	14. B	19. C
5. C	10. C	15. B	20. A

CHAPTER 10
Emotional Development

You Should Know:

Introduction

- how Mischel predicted long-term outcomes from childhood behavior.
- how emotional intelligence differs from IQ, and why it is important.

The Development of Emotions in Childhood (*summary on pg. 383 of text*)

Introduction
- how "emotions" differ from "feelings".
- the components of emotions.

Theories on the Nature and Emergence of Emotion
- how researchers and theorists differ on the innate versus learned nature of emotions, the association between emotions and facial expressions, and the developmental progression of emotional experience.

The Emergence of Emotion in the Early Years and Childhood
- the general developmental progression of the experience and expression of positive emotions and negative emotions.
- how infants' emotions are assessed in the laboratory, and what research has indicated about the differentiation of negative emotions in infancy.
- how separation anxiety differs across environments.
- how self-conscious emotions differ from other emotions, in terms of their characteristics and their development.
- how caregivers can encourage children to experience guilt over shame.
- how the causes and experience of emotions differ across childhood and adolescence.

Box 10.1: Gender Differences in Adolescent Depression
- how rates with which adolescents experience depression differ across boys and girls and the possible causes of these differences.

Regulation of Emotion (*summary on pg. 387 of text*)

The Development of Emotional Regulation

- what emotional regulation entails, and how infants and young children begin to regulate their own emotions.
- how older children regulate their emotions differently than do younger children, and why older children's selection of strategies differs from that of younger children.

The Relation of Emotional Regulation to Social Competence and Adjustment

- how and why emotional regulation is associated with social competence and adjustment.

Individual Differences in Emotion and Its Regulation (*summary on pg. 394 of text*)

Temperament

- what temperament is and how Thomas and Chess, as well as more recent researchers, have characterized infants and children.
- how early temperament is associated with later temperament and later adjustment.
- how the environment combines with a child's temperament to affect later outcomes.

Box 10.2: Measurement of Temperament

- the multiple ways in which temperament has been assessed and the advantages and disadvantages of the various methods.
- what behavioral inhibition is, how it has been assessed, and how it is associated with later behavioral patterns.

Children's Emotional Development in the Family (*summary on pg. 399 of text*)

Introduction

- how temperament and personality are related.

Quality of the Child's Relationships with Parents

- the ways in which the quality of the parent-child relationship is associated with emotional development.

Parental Socialization of Children's Emotional Responding

- the ways in which parents have a direct and indirect influence on their children's emotional response.
- how parents' expression of emotion, parents' reactions to children's emotions, and parental conversations about emotions are associated with children's emotional responding and later adjustment.
- how children's own behavior may affect parents' expression of emotion, parents' reactions to children's emotions, and parental conversations about emotions.

Box 10.3: Gender Differences in the Expression of Emotion
- how girls and boys differ in their expression of emotion and how this varies across cultures.
- why girls and boys may differ in their emotional expression.

Culture and Children's Emotional Development (*summary on pg. 401 of text*)

- how the expression of emotion varies across cultures and subcultures and how this is associated with cultural differences in parenting practices and cultural values.

Children's Understanding of Emotion (*summary on pg. 408 of text*)

Identifying the Emotions of Others
- the developmental progression of children's ability to identify others' emotions and why this is an important skill.
- how the ability to identify emotions has been studied.

Understanding the Causes of Emotion
- the developmental progression of children's understanding of emotions and why this is an important skill.
- how the understanding of emotions has generally been studied and the problems with this methodology.

Children's Understanding of Real and False Emotions
- the developmental progression of children's understanding of real and false emotions.
- how social factors influence children's understanding of real and false emotions.

Children's Understanding of Simultaneous and Ambivalent Emotions
- the developmental progression of children's understanding of simultaneous and ambivalent emotions.

Key Term Matching I: Definitions

Instructions: Match each key term with its definition.

KEY TERM

1. _____ personality
2. _____ self-conscious emotions
3. _____ goodness of fit
4. _____ discrete emotions theory
5. _____ social referencing
6. _____ temperament
7. _____ emotion
8. _____ socialization

9. _____ behavioral inhibition
10. _____ separation anxiety
11. _____ social competence
12. _____ display rules
13. _____ emotional intelligence
14. _____ emotional self-regulation
15. _____ social smiles
16. _____ functionalist approach

DEFINITION

a. the pattern of emotional and behavioral tendencies, beliefs and interests, and intellectual capabilities that characterize an individual

b. a social group's informal norms about when, where, and how much one should show emotions

c. the view that emotions are distinct from one another and are evident from early in life

d. differences in aspects of emotional, motor, and attention reactivity and self-regulation that are apparent from early in life

e. the degree to which an individual's temperament is suited to their particular environment

f. feeling of distress that infants experience when separated from an attachment figure

g. emotions that relate to an individual's sense of self and an awareness of others' reactions

h. the process of controlling one's emotions, including the associated subjective feelings, physiological processes, behaviors, and cognitions

i. the ability to achieve one's goals in social situations while maintaining positive relations with others

j. the view that the purpose of emotions is to promote action toward a goal

k. a dimension of temperament that involves fearful distress, particularly in novel situations

l. smiles that are directed at people

m. a set of abilities that are key to competent social functioning

n. the indirect and direct influences of parents, teachers, and other aspects of the environment on children's standards, values, and ways of thinking and feeling

o. infants' use of a caregiver's facial or vocal cues to interpret a novel or ambiguous situation

p. characterized by a motivational force, subjective experience, changes in physiology, and cognitions

Key Term Matching II: Applications, Examples, and More

Instructions: Match each key term with an application or example of the term.

KEY TERM

1. _____ separation anxiety
2. _____ emotional intelligence
3. _____ social smiles
4. _____ personality
5. _____ discrete emotions theory
6. _____ display rules
7. _____ socialization
8. _____ self-conscious emotions

9. _____ goodness of fit
10. _____ emotion
11. _____ social competence
12. _____ behavioral inhibition
13. _____ functionalist approach
14. _____ social referencing
15. _____ emotional self-regulation
16. _____ temperament

APPLICATION OR EXAMPLE

a. these emerge as early as 6 or 7 weeks of age and do not refer to happiness experienced as a result of being able to control an object

b. children who have a high activity level, have intense reactions to negative stimuli, and are not easily distractible and children who are generally cheerful and easy to calm differ in this

c. when infants begin to do this at about 8 to 12 months of age, it is an indication that they can relate others' emotional expressions to events in the environment

d. researchers holding this view would point to the association between anger and an individual's movement to eliminate obstacles

e. this predicts how well individuals do in life even to a greater extent than does IQ

f. a child who crawls away from his caregiver is probably less likely to experience this than a child whose caregiver leaves the room

g. happiness, anger, and sadness are <u>not</u> examples of these

h. young children who must rely on caregivers to settle them down have not fully developed this

i. this has its roots in temperament, but is also shaped by the environment

j. theorists disagree about the extent to which this involves cognition as well as whether the experience of this is entirely innate or partially learned

k.   infants who are high in this tend to be less social and less positive at age four

l.   even a child with a difficult temperament can thrive if the environment is satisfactory in terms of this

m.   children with this are good at regulating their emotions, tend to use cognitive methods of controlling their emotions, and tend to be able to delay gratification

n.   parents' expression of emotion with their children and parents' reactions to their children's emotional expression are two examples of how parents accomplish this

o.   researchers holding this view would <u>disagree</u> with the statement, "Infants only experience excitement and distress, and they must learn how to express these emotions"

p.   examples of these include those with a prosocial motive, when one doesn't want to hurt another's feelings, and those with a self-protective motive, when one doesn't want to look bad in front of others

Multiple-Choice Questions

1. Emotional intelligence includes:
    A. the ability to regulate one's emotions.
    B. the ability to delay gratification.
    C. knowledge about what makes people experience various emotions.
    D. the ability to identify one's own emotional state.
    E. A and D
    F. all of the above

2. Young infants tend to smile at all of the following except:
    A. at people.
    B. at interesting objects.
    C. when they can control an event.
    D. Young infants tend to smile at all of the above.

3. Which of the following children is least likely to experience separation anxiety?
    A. 11-month-old Tara, who crawls away from her mother to explore a novel toy.
    B. 10-month-old Lee, whose mother leaves him in his crib.
    C. 13-month-old Bethany, who is blind and hears her mother leave the room.
    D. 6-month-old Simon, whose mother leaves the room in which he is playing.
    E. All of these children are equally likely to experience separation anxiety.
    F. Tara (A) and Simon (D) are both unlikely to experience separation anxiety.
    G. Bethany (C) and Simon (D) are both unlikely to experience separation anxiety.

4. Which of the following is not a self-conscious emotion?
    A. pride
    B. shame
    C. embarrassment
    D. fear

5. Juan is jumping on the bed and mistakenly falls and kicks his sister. He feels terrible and regrets jumping on the bed. He is trying desperately to make her feel better by hugging and kissing her. Juan is primarily experiencing which of the following emotions?
    A. anger
    B. embarrassment
    C. guilt
    D. shame

6. Which of the following is a true statement about rates of depression and negative emotion in childhood and adolescence?
   A. Typical adolescents experience only a mild increase in negative emotions.
   B. Rates of clinical depression are very high during childhood.
   C. Changes in emotionality during adolescence are entirely due to hormonal changes.
   D. Rates of depression do not change from childhood to adolescence.
   E. none of the above

7. As children get older, they increasingly regulate their negative emotions by:
   A. relying on their parents.
   B. using cognitive strategies.
   C. having temper tantrums.
   D. using more physical self-soothing techniques.

8. Thomas and Chess labeled babies who were generally cheerful, who adjusted to new situations without much trouble, and who were regular in their routines as:
   A. slow-to-warm-up.
   B. difficult.
   C. easy.
   D. quick-to-calm-down.

9. Infants' anger and frustration, especially when being prevented from doing what they want is referred to as:
   A. surgency.
   B. irritable distress.
   C. rhythmicity.
   D. fearful distress.
   E. low positive affect.

10. Children high in fearful distress, particularly in novel or stressful situations, are considered to be:
   A. behaviorally inhibited.
   B. irritable.
   C. high in anger/frustration.
   D. easy.

11. Children with behavioral inhibition are more likely than children with other temperaments to exhibit which of the following as adolescents or young adults?
   A. popularity
   B. getting in trouble with the law
   C. impulsivity
   D. anxiety

12. Goodness of fit describes which of the following associations?
   A. the effect of children's temperament on later social functioning
   B. the interaction between children's temperament and their social (e.g., family) environment
   C. the effect of family environment on children's temperament
   D. the interaction between children's temperamental regulation and their temperamental emotionality

13. Which of the following is <u>not</u> a true statement about gender differences and the expression of emotion?
   A. Gender differences in emotional expression are consistent across cultures.
   B. Boys display more anger than do girls.
   C. Males and females display different patterns of emotion as early as infancy.
   D. Parents display more positive emotion with their daughters than with their sons.

14. A nine-month-old infant is habituated to pictures of people expressing happiness. The infant is then presented with a picture of a person expressing anger. The infant is likely to:
   A. display no renewed interest in the pictures, as infants this young are unable to differentiate between emotions.
   B. dishabituate to the new picture, but not comprehend the difference in meaning between the first set of pictures and the new picture.
   C. dishabituate to the new picture and comprehend the emotional meaning of the facial expressions.
   D. cry, as the removal of the happy face is likely to elicit fear in the infant.

15. Children's use of a parent's facial, vocal, or gestural cues to decide on how to deal with ambiguous situations is referred to as:
   A. social referencing.
   B. emotional regulation.
   C. self-socialization.
   D. display rules.

16. Does social referencing involve infants' emotional <u>and</u> behavioral responses to ambiguous events?
   A. Yes, it involves <u>both</u> emotional and behavioral responses.
   B. No, it involves emotional responses, but not behavioral responses.
   C. No, it involves behavioral responses, but not emotional responses.
   D. No, it involves <u>neither</u> emotional nor behavioral responses.

17. Three-year-old Ian is told a story about Jimmy, a boy who loves to go to the park. Jimmy is in the car with his father, and they are on their way to the park. When Ian is asked how Jimmy is feeling, Ian is likely to expect which of the following emotions?
   A. sadness
   B. shame
   C. happiness
   D. Ian will be unable to predict Jimmy's emotion.

18. Which of the following is an ability of the typical fifth grader?
   A. identifying the causes of others' negative emotions
   B. labeling self-conscious emotions in other people
   C. identifying the causes of others' positive emotions
   D. a good understanding of how memories of past emotional events can trigger the same emotions
   E. all of the above
   F. none of the above

19. Which of the following is <u>not</u> an example of the use of a display rule?
   A. Sam pretends to be happy when he takes a bite of his friend's cooking concoction.
   B. Nilda appears sad when her friend is leaving even though she is relieved to have her go.
   C. Ross is excited about making a mess in his playroom but gets upset when his mother comes in the room and gets angry.
   D. Emma smiles in front of her classmates even though she has just lost the spelling bee.

20. Which of the following children's emotions would be the <u>most difficult</u> for other children to understand?
   A. Mia, who feels disappointment at getting a sweater for her birthday, but who puts on a happy face anyway.
   B. J.T, who feels sad at a happy occasion (e.g., birthday party).
   C. Kerry, who is saddened by a reminder of her pets' death.
   D. Jing, who is happy because he is going to the park with his friend.

Essay Questions

Instructions: Answer the following essay questions on a separate sheet of paper.

1. Describe the impact of the sociocultural context on the development and experience of emotions, including basic emotions and self-conscious emotions. Provide supportive examples.

2. Describe an event that would evoke fear in children of each of the following ages: infancy, toddlerhood, preschool age, and late childhood. Describe how children of each of these ages would be likely to attempt to regulate their fear.

3. Think about an infant you know or use the information your parents have told you about what you were like as an infant. Would the parents of this infant describe the infant (or you) as an easy, difficult, or slow-to-warm-up child? What characteristics does this infant exhibit that cause you to classify him or her in that way?

4. Describe the three ways that parents socialize their children's emotional development. Give an example of each. In addition, for each of the three paths, give an example of how children may influence their parents.

5. Why is it so important for social competence that children can identify their own emotions? In addition, why is it so important for social competence that children can identify other people's emotions? Provide supportive examples.

Answer Key

Key Term Matching I

1. a	4. c	7. p	10. f	13. m	16. j
2. g	5. o	8. n	11. i	14. h	
3. e	6. d	9. k	12. b	15. l	

Key Term Matching II

1. f	4. i	7. n	10. j	13. d	16. b
2. e	5. o	8. g	11. m	14. c	
3. a	6. p	9. l	12. k	15. h	

Multiple-Choice Questions

1. F	6. A	11. D	16. A
2. D	7. B	12. B	17. C
3. F	8. C	13. A	18. E
4. D	9. B	14. C	19. C
5. C	10. A	15. A	20. A

CHAPTER 11
Attachment to Others and Development of Self

You Should Know:

Introduction

- the types of observations child-care professionals were making in the 1930s and 1940s of children growing up in institutions and foster care.
- how these observations and early research changed the predominant view of the important dimensions of caregiving and sparked the important writings of John Bowlby.

The Caregiver-Child Attachment Relationship (*summary on pg. 424 of text*)

Introduction
- what early research was conducted on issues of attachment and early social interaction and how the findings informed future research.

Attachment Theory
- Bowlby's conception of attachment and how the caregiver is regarded in his attachment theory.
- the phases through which attachment is proposed to develop and what the usual outcome of these phases is.

Measurement of Attachment Security
- the general features of the most commonly-used laboratory test for assessing infants' attachment to their primary caregiver and why Ainsworth believed these features were important in the assessment of attachment behavior.
- what infant behaviors are observed during the Strange Situation and how infants are categorized into attachment groups according to this behavior.

Box 11.1: Parental Attachment Status
- what adult attachment models are and how they are assessed.
- how parents' attachment classification is associated with their children's attachment style and why these associations exist.

Cultural Variations in Attachment

- how attachment patterns are similar across cultures, as well as how they differ.

- why the behavior of infants in the Strange Situation may differ across cultures and what the possible explanations for these differences are.

Factors Associated with the Security of Children's Attachment

- why parental sensitivity is believed to be crucial to the development of a secure attachment and how mothers of securely attached infants and mothers of insecurely-attached infants differ.

- what role infants' own temperament plays in their attachment style.

Box 11.2: Interventions and Attachment

- why interventions enable researchers to examine the causal nature of parental sensitivity on infant attachment, as well as what intervention research has demonstrated about this issue.

Does Security of Attachment Have Long-Term Effects?

- how attachment style in infancy is associated with later psychological, social, and cognitive functioning.

- what controversy exists about whether this association is a causal one, what research has been done to examine this issue, and what this research has demonstrated.

Conceptions of the Self (*summary on pg. 435 of text*)

Introduction

- what the self is and why the development of conceptions of the self is important to psychological functioning.

The Development of Conceptions of Self

- how a sense of self emerges throughout the first three years of life and what empirical evidence has informed psychologists' understanding of this development.

- how children and adolescents of different ages typically describe themselves and what this reflects about their conceptions of self.

- what developmental changes influence the development of children's and adolescents' conceptions of self.

- how adolescents' egocentrism influences their beliefs about themselves.

Box 11.3: Conceptions of the Self and Children's Achievement Motivation

- the different patterns exhibited by children when they are faced with failure at a task.

- how children's theories of intelligence and success are associated with these differences in children's responses to failure.

- how parents influence children's orientation toward learning and what can be done to help children who exhibit a helpless pattern.

Identity in Adolescence

- Erikson's conception of identity formation, the types of negative outcomes that are possible in this process, and why Erikson believed in the importance of a psychosocial moratorium.
- how research on identity formation has followed from Erikson's theory and what identity statuses have been identified.
- how individuals' identity status is associated with their functioning.
- how identity formation is influenced by parenting behavior, adolescents' own behavior, and the larger culture.

Ethnic Identity (*summary on pg. 438 of text*)

Ethnic Identity in Childhood

- the components of ethnic identity and how ethnic identity develops during childhood.

Ethnic Identity in Adolescence

- how the development of identity for ethnic-minority youth differs from that of ethnic-majority youth.
- the common pattern of ethnic-identity development, as well as the likely outcomes of this process.

Sexual Identity or Orientation (*summary on pg. 442 of text*)

The Origins of Youths' Sexual Identity

- how heredity and environment influence the development of sexual identity.

Sexual Identity in Sexual-Minority Youth

- the challenges many sexual-minority youth face in the development of a sexual identity.
- the developmental milestones of the coming-out process.
- what the consequences of coming out may be for the family and peer relationships of sexual-minority youth.

Self-Esteem (*summary on pg. 447 of text*)

Sources of Self-Esteem

- how parents and peers influence children's self-esteem differently depending on the age of the child.
- how children's appearance and competence in different domains, as well as children's school organization and neighborhood, are associated with self-esteem.

Self-Esteem in Minority Children

- the patterns of self-esteem for ethnic-minority children and how they compare to those of ethnic-majority children.

Culture and Self-Esteem

- how the form of self-esteem, as well as its sources, differs across cultures.

Key Term Matching I: Definitions

Instructions: Match each key term with its definition.

Set A

KEY TERM

1. _____ imaginary audience
2. _____ self
3. _____ moratorium status
4. _____ identity-achievement status
5. _____ adult attachment models
6. _____ Strange Situation
7. _____ identity-diffusion status
8. _____ helpless pattern of motivation

9. _____ foreclosure status
10. _____ personal fable
11. _____ attachment theory
12. _____ insecure attachment
13. _____ social comparison
14. _____ mastery-oriented pattern of motivation
15. _____ secure attachment
16. _____ identity versus identity confusion

DEFINITION

a.   Erikson's psychosocial stage of development that occurs during adolescence in which the crisis involves the construction of a coherent identity

b.   a method developed by Mary Ainsworth to assess infants' attachments to their primary caregivers

c.   adolescents' belief that they, and especially their feelings, are unique and special

d.   a pattern of attachment in which a child has a relatively poor-quality relationship with the attachment figure

e.   a response to failure in which individuals feel badly, blame themselves, and do not persist at the task because they believe they cannot succeed

f.   a conceptual system consisting of one's thoughts and attitudes about oneself

g.   the process of judging oneself against the psychological, behavioral, or physical functioning of others in order to evaluate oneself

h.   working models of attachment relationships that guide parents' attachments with their own children and are believed to be based on their perceptions of their own childhood experiences

i.   the identity-status category in which an individual does not have any firm commitments but is exploring various options

j.   a pattern of attachment in which a child has a high-quality relationship with the attachment figure

k.   the identity-status category in which an individual has explored various options and has made an autonomous commitment to personal decisions such as ideology, occupation, and sexual behavior

l.   a theory that hypothesizes that children are biologically predisposed to form attachments with their caregivers as a means of increasing their chances of survival

m.   the identity-status category in which an individual does not have any firm commitments and is not making progress toward them

n.   the identity-status category in which an individual has not engaged in any identity exploration and has established an identity based on the choices or values of others

o.   a response to failure in which individuals try harder to succeed at the task and do not feel negatively about themselves

p.   adolescents' belief that everyone else is focused on the adolescent's appearance and behavior

Set B

KEY TERM

17. _____   negative identity

18. _____   parental sensitivity

19. _____   identity confusion

20. _____   self-esteem

21. _____   insecure/avoidant attachment

22. _____   secure base

23. _____   disorganized/disoriented attachment

24. _____   internal working model of attachment

25. _____   sexual orientation

26. _____   attachment

27. _____   psychosocial moratorium

28. _____   ethnic identity

29. _____   identity foreclosure

30. _____   sexual-minority youth

31. _____   insecure/resistant attachment

DEFINITION

q.   close, enduring emotional bond with a specific person

r.   the notion that an attachment figure's presence provides a child with a sense of safety and confidence that enables the child to explore the environment

s.   a crucial factor contributing to the security of an infant's attachment that includes responsive caregiving when children are distressed

t.   an identity that represents the opposite of what is valued by people around the adolescent

u.   a time-out period in which an adolescent can explore activities that lead to self-discovery without having to take on any adult roles

v.   a pattern of attachment in which a child appears to have no consistent way of coping with the Strange Situation and thus behaves in a confused or contradictory manner

w.   a mental representation of the self, of attachment figures, and of relationships in general that is a result of experiences with caregivers

x.   an incomplete and sometimes incoherent sense of self that results from an unsuccessful resolution of Erikson's identity versus identity-confusion stage

y.   premature commitment to an identity without adequately considering other choices

z.   a pattern of attachment in which a child is clingy and stays close to the caregiver rather than exploring the environment

aa.   young individuals who experience same-sex attractions

bb.   an individual's sense of belonging to an ethnic group

cc.   an individual's preference in regard to males or females as the object of erotic feelings

dd.   a pattern of attachment in which a child appears to be indifferent towards the caregiver and may stay away from the caregiver

ee.   one's overall evaluation of the worth of the self and the feelings associated with that evaluation

Key Term Matching II: Applications, Examples, and More

Instructions: Match each key term with an application or example of the term.

Set A

KEY TERM

1. _____   social comparison

2. _____   Strange Situation

3. _____   identity-achievement status

4. _____   identity-diffusion status

5. _____   self

6. _____   attachment theory

7. _____   moratorium status

8. _____   mastery-oriented pattern of motivation

9. _____   personal fable

10. _____   imaginary audience

11. _____   adult attachment models

12. _____   foreclosure status

13. _____   helpless pattern of motivation

14. _____   secure attachment

APPLICATION OR EXAMPLE

a.   children who demonstrate this tend to believe that their failure is a result of insufficient effort or lack of preparation and thus that trying harder will result in success

b.   individuals with this identity status tend to believe that authority figures should make decisions for them

c.   children who exhibited this pattern of attachment as infants tend to have closer, more harmonious relationships with their peers than do other children

d.   this is generally assessed by asking adults to discuss their early childhood attachments and how they believe those early relationships have shaped them

e.   this belief causes adolescents to be preoccupied with what others think of them

f.   elementary-school children's engagement in this causes them to refine their conceptions of self to include attention to discrepancies between their own and others' behavior and characteristics

g.   Carol Dweck and her colleagues have suggested that this reflects individuals' beliefs that intelligence is a fixed trait and that it cannot be changed

h.   this theory was proposed by John Bowlby

i. individuals with this identity status tend to be high in self-esteem and high in anxiety, and they tend to move into identity-achievement status

j. in modern, Western cultures, individuals who have attained this identity status tend to be more socially mature and more highly motivated than their peers

k. individuals with this identity status tend to be the most at-risk for drug abuse

l. during this, the infant's behaviors, including attempts to seek closeness with the caregiver, resistance to or avoidance of the caregiver, and interactions with the caregiver from a distance, are observed

m. an adolescent who says to his or her parents, "But you don't understand how it feels to be a teenager," is demonstrating this form of egocentrism

n. an emerging understanding of this is apparent when a child succeeds at the "rouge test" and makes movements toward wiping the spot off of his or her own face rather than off of the image in the mirror

Set B

KEY TERM

15. _____ psychosocial moratorium

16. _____ sexual-minority youth

17. _____ parental sensitivity

18. _____ insecure/avoidant attachment

19. _____ attachment

20. _____ identity foreclosure

21. _____ internal working model of attachment

22. _____ identity confusion

23. _____ self-esteem

24. _____ negative identity

25. _____ insecure/resistant attachment

26. _____ ethnic identity

27. _____ secure base

28. _____ disorganized/disoriented attachment

APPLICATION OR EXAMPLE

o.   a child whose caregiver does not serve this function may be unable to fully explore the environment, thereby decreasing opportunities for learning

p.   Erikson argued for the importance of this in modern society because of the complexity of achieving an identity

q.   parents who do not read their infants' signals correctly and do not respond appropriately to a baby who is crying versus smiling would be considered to be low in this

r.   the mothers of infants who display this pattern of attachment have been found to be inconsistent in their caregiving and are often anxious or overwhelmed

s.   in the Strange Situation, infants with this pattern of attachment often ignore their caregivers when they enter the room following a separation episode and ignore or turn away from them when they are in the room

t.   although it is often assumed that minority children have poorer _____ than majority children, this is generally not the case, perhaps because of minority cultures' strong and positive ethnic identity

u.   as a result of this, if children's caregivers are unresponsive and unavailable, children may hold negative perceptions of themselves and may believe that all relationships will be negative and unfulfilling

v.   this includes the degree to which individuals associate their thinking, perceptions, feelings, and behavior with membership in their ethnic group

w.   an example of this is an individual who becomes a minister simply because his parent is one

x.   adolescents in this state often feel lost, isolated, or depressed

y.   the security of this appears to have many short- and long-term consequences for children's adjustment

z.   this attachment category is often associated with a history of parental abuse

aa.   for these individuals, the question of personal sexual identity is often confusing and painful

bb.   Erikson believed the adoption of this is some adolescents' means of getting noticed by their parents when other attempts have failed

Multiple-Choice Questions

1. Bowlby proposed that newborns are in which phase of the development of attachment?
   A. attachment-in-the-making
   B. clear-cut attachment
   C. preattachment
   D. reciprocal relationships

2. Bowlby proposed that individuals' internal working models of attachment include mental representations of:
   A. attachment figures.
   B. the self.
   C. relationships in general.
   D. A and B
   E. A and C
   F. all of the above

3. Which of the following behaviors during the Strange Situation is <u>not</u> characteristic of securely attached infants?
   A. playing alone with the toys in the room
   B. easily comforted by mother when upset
   C. distress when mother leaves the room
   D. failure to greet mother when she returns to the room
   E. Both C and D are uncharacteristic of securely attached infants.

4. Adults' working models of attachment are:
   A. based on adults' perceptions of their own childhood experiences.
   B. assessed by observing adults with their own parents.
   C. only held by adults who had secure attachments to their own parents.
   D. unrelated to their children's attachments to them.

5. Which of the following can have an impact on infants' behavior in the Strange Situation?
   A. cultural value placed on infants' dependency on their mothers
   B. childrearing practices
   C. prior experience with unfamiliar people and situations
   D. A and B
   E. B and C
   F. all of the above

6. Mothers who are able to read their infants' signals and respond to them appropriately are likely to have infants who are:
   A. depressed.
   B. securely attached.
   C. slow-to-warm-up.
   D. disorganized/disoriented.

7. Which of the following is a true statement about the long-term association between security of attachment in infancy and later social and emotional competence?
   A. There is a clear causal long-term association.
   B. There is some evidence that the association is causal, but there is also evidence that current attachment security is the relevant factor.
   C. It is clear that the association is not a causal one.
   D. There is a clear causal association, but only over short periods of time.

8. Which of the following is <u>not</u> an indication of a child's sense of self?
   A. separation distress
   B. anger at loss of control of movement of a mobile
   C. crying when hungry
   D. attempting to engage adults by handing them objects

9. Children who attempt to wipe the rouge off their own face when they are asked to clean the face of the child in the mirror:
   A. are demonstrating that they possess a sense of self.
   B. are securely attached to their primary caregiver.
   C. have a great deal of experience with make-up.
   D. have higher self-esteem than other children.

10. Which of the following is more likely to be a characteristic of a ten-year-old child's sense of self than a five-year-old child's sense of self?
    A. focused on observable characteristics
    B. involves others' evaluations of them
    C. closely tied to actual behavior
    D. based on physical attributes

11. Children who blame themselves for failure, feel badly when they fail, and do not persist when they are failing at a task are referred to as displaying:
    A. poor academic competence.
    B. a mastery orientation.
    C. an insecure attachment.
    D. a helpless pattern of motivation.

12. At what age do the inconsistencies people perceive in their personalities start to bother them?
   A. early childhood
   B. late childhood
   C. early adolescence
   D. adolescence

13. Owen is an adolescent who doesn't know who he is or what he wants to make of his life. He feels isolated and depressed. Erikson would say that Owen:
   A. has a negative identity.
   B. is in a state of identity confusion.
   C. is experiencing identity foreclosure.
   D. is in a state of moratorium.
   E. has a coherent identity.

14. A period in which an adolescent can discover herself and not be expected to take on adult roles is referred to as a(n):
   A. state of identity confusion.
   B. identity achievement.
   C. moratorium.
   D. foreclosed identity.
   E. negative identity.

15. Research has indicated that adolescents in which of the following states are most at risk for drug abuse?
   A. identity diffusion
   B. moratorium
   C. foreclosure
   D. identity achievement

16. At what age do individuals start to develop meaningful ethnic labels (e.g., "I'm Mexican because my parents come from Mexico)?
   A. preschool
   B. early childhood
   C. late childhood/early adolescence
   D. early adulthood

17. Individuals' preferences in regard to males or females as the objects of erotic feelings are referred to as their:
   A. ethnic identity.
   B. identity achievement.
   C. gender identity.
   D. sexual orientation.
   E. gender role.

18. Which of the following is not common for sexual-minority individuals?
   A. confidence in disclosing sexual orientation to friends and family
   B. parental anger and disappointment
   C. lack of peer acceptance of sexual orientation
   D. increased rate of attempted suicide

19. How are peer acceptance and children's self-esteem associated?
   A. Children's self-esteem influences how well-accepted they are by their peers.
   B. Children's peer acceptance influences their self-esteem.
   C. both A and B
   D. neither A nor B

20. Which of the following is not a true statement about the self-esteem of ethnic minority children in comparison to Euro-American children?
   A. The self-esteem of some ethnic minorities is negatively affected by the increased prevalence of living in poverty.
   B. The self-esteem of some ethnic minorities is negatively affected by their strong ethnic identity.
   C. The self-esteem of some ethnic minorities is positively affected by their parents' encouragement of closeness and connection with the family.
   D. The reported self-esteem of some ethnic minorities is relatively low due to their cultural motivation toward being self-critical.
   E. All of the above are true statements.

Essay Questions

Instructions: Answer the following essay questions on a separate sheet of paper.

1. What is strange about the Strange Situation? Why is this situation so effective in assessing the quality of infant-caregiver security?

2. What is a sense of self? Describe three indicators that a child has developed a sense of self. Provide examples of each.

3. Describe Erikson's concept of identity. What is a successful identity? Give an example of an adolescent who has achieved this state. Also, describe and give an example of an individual in each of the following identity states: (1) identity confusion, (2) identity foreclosure, (3) negative identity, and (4) moratorium.

4. How does sociocultural context influence the coming-out process and its consequences for sexual-minority youth? Give three supportive examples.

5. Describe how an individual's identity is associated with his or her self-esteem. Are these concepts the same thing? Why or why not?

Answer Key

Key Term Matching I

1.	p	6.	b	11.	l	16.	a	21.	dd	26.	q	31. z
2.	f	7.	m	12.	d	17.	t	22.	r	27.	u	
3.	i	8.	e	13.	g	18.	s	23.	v	28.	bb	
4.	k	9.	n	14.	o	19.	x	24.	w	29.	y	
5.	h	10.	c	15.	j	20.	ee	25.	cc	30.	aa	

Key Term Matching II

1.	f	5.	n	9.	m	13.	g	17.	q	21.	u	25.	r
2.	l	6.	h	10.	e	14.	c	18.	s	22.	x	26.	v
3.	j	7.	i	11.	d	15.	p	19.	y	23.	t	27.	o
4.	k	8.	a	12.	b	16.	aa	20.	w	24.	bb	28.	z

Multiple-Choice Questions

1.	C	6.	B	11.	D	16.	B
2.	F	7.	B	12.	D	17.	D
3.	D	8.	C	13.	B	18.	A
4.	A	9.	A	14.	C	19.	C
5.	F	10.	B	15.	A	20.	B

CHAPTER 12
The Family

You Should Know:

Introduction

- what researchers have learned about the relation between family structure and children's development by examining families affected by the one-child policy in China.

The Nature and Functions of the Family *(summary on pg. 455 of text)*

Functions of Families
- what functions of families are common across all societies.

Family Dynamics
- what is meant by family dynamics and what relationships are involved, both within the family and from outside the family.
- what the implications of understanding the complexity of family dynamics are for conducting research on families.

Box 12.1: Parent-Child Relationships in Adolescence
- how parent-child relationships tend to change and how they tend to remain the same as children become adolescents.

The Influence of Parental Socialization *(summary on pg. 467 of text)*

Introduction
- the ways in which parents can influence their children's development through socialization.

Parenting Styles and Practices
- the dimensions on which parents can differ in terms of their behavior and attitudes that can influence the pattern of parent-child interactions.
- what parenting styles have been identified by Baumrind, including the parenting behaviors and attitudes characteristic of each style and the common outcomes for children of each style.
- how the outcomes associated with different parenting styles and practices can differ in different subcultures and cultures.

The Child as an Influence on Parenting

- how children's physical attractiveness can influence parental behavior.
- how children's behavior and temperaments may influence parental behavior and how the bidirectionality of parent-child interactions can support and maintain parents' and children's behavior.

Box 12.2: Child Maltreatment by Parents

- what is meant by child maltreatment and what types of maltreatment exist.
- what factors are related to child maltreatment and what interventions may be effective in reducing its likelihood.
- how child maltreatment appears to affect children's development.

Socioeconomic Influences on Parenting

- how parents who differ in socioeconomic status differ in parenting style and practices and what beliefs, values, and environmental factors appear to contribute to these differences.
- how economic stress and poverty are related to the quality of parenting and family interactions and how social support can diminish some of these effects.

Box 12.3: Homelessness

- the likely impact of homelessness on children's and adolescents' adjustment.

Mothers, Fathers, and Siblings (*summary on pg. 470 of text*)

Differences in Mothers' and Fathers' Interactions with Their Children

- how the degree of involvement in parenting and parent-child interactions differ for mothers and fathers.

Sibling Relationships

- how siblings can influence one another's development for better and for worse.
- what factors play a role in whether or not siblings get along with one another, as well as what parents can do to increase the likelihood of positive interactions among their children.

Changes in Families in the United States (*summary on pg. 482 of text*)

Introduction

- how the family in the United States has changed during the past 50 years.

Older Parents

- how differences in the resources of younger and older parents relate to differences in their parenting practices.
- how older parents differ from younger parents in their attitudes about parenting.

Box 12.4: Adolescents as Parents
- what factors increase and decrease the likelihood that teenagers will become parents.
- the apparent consequences of adolescent parenting for the adolescent and the child.
- what factors influence whether the father will be involved and what the consequences of his involvement appear to be for the child.

Divorce
- what the research suggests are the consequences of divorce for children and the likelihood that they will experience significant, enduring problems.
- what factors appear to influence the impact of divorce on children.
- what types of custody arrangements exist and how experts believe these influence children's adjustment.
- how the correlates of divorce compare to the effects of ongoing marital conflict.

Stepparenting
- the characteristics of typical stepparent-child relationships and what appears to influence whether these relationships will be positive or negative.
- how the age and sex of the child and the parenting behaviors of both the custodial parent and the stepparent are related to children's adjustment in stepfamilies.

Lesbian and Gay Parents
- how children of gay and lesbian parents compare to children of heterosexual parents.
- how family dynamics appear to influence the adjustment of children of gay and lesbian parents.

Maternal Employment and Child Care (*summary on pg. 489 of text*)

Introduction
- how the employment rate for mothers of children of different ages has changed over the past several decades.

The Effects of Maternal Employment
- how maternal employment when children are infants appears to influence infants' development.
- how maternal employment appears to influence children's development both positively and negatively and the child and parent factors that appear to affect whether the impact is positive or negative.

The Effects of Child Care

- what types of child care are common in the U.S.

- how child care is associated with attachment and the parent-child relationship and how the quality and amount of child care may contribute to this influence.

- how child care is associated with children's social, cognitive, and language development and how the quality and amount of child care may contribute to these associations.

- the characteristics of high-quality child care programs.

Key Term Matching I: Definitions

Instructions: Match each key term with its definition.

KEY TERM

1. _____ survival of offspring
2. _____ rejecting-neglecting parenting
3. _____ authoritative parenting
4. _____ family dynamics
5. _____ socialization
6. _____ parenting styles
7. _____ cultural training

8. _____ authoritarian parenting
9. _____ bidirectionality of parent-child interactions
10. _____ economic function
11. _____ child maltreatment
12. _____ permissive parenting
13. _____ complex stepfamilies

DEFINITION

a. parenting behaviors and attitudes that set the emotional climate of parent-child interactions

b. a function of the family; pertains to providing the means for children to acquire the skills and other resources they need to be economically productive adults

c. the process through which children acquire the values, standards, skills, knowledge, and behaviors that are appropriate for their role in their culture

d. a parenting style that is high in demandingness and low in responsiveness

e. intentional abuse or neglect that endangers anyone under the age of 18

f. a function of the family; pertains to ensuring that children survive by attending to their needs

g. a parenting style that is high in both demandingness and responsiveness

h. the notion that parents' characteristics and behavior affect children's characteristics and behavior and vice versa

i. a parenting style that is low in demandingness and high in responsiveness

j. a function of the family; pertains to teaching children the basic values in their culture

k. families that contain half siblings or stepsiblings

l. a parenting style that is low in both demandingness and responsiveness

m. the way in which the family operates as a whole

Key Term Matching II: Applications, Examples, and More

Instructions: Match each key term with an application or example of the term.

KEY TERM

1. _____ authoritative parenting
2. _____ economic function
3. _____ rejecting-neglecting parenting
4. _____ family dynamics
5. _____ socialization
6. _____ parenting styles
7. _____ survival of offspring

8. _____ authoritarian parenting
9. _____ cultural training
10. _____ bidirectionality of parent-child interactions
11. _____ permissive parenting
12. _____ complex stepfamilies
13. _____ child maltreatment

APPLICATION OR EXAMPLE

a.   the most fundamental function of the family

b.   parents who exhibit this tend to be focused on their own needs rather than on their children, and their children are at-risk for a host of problem behaviors, including substance abuse, internalizing problems, and promiscuous sexual behavior

c.   in the U.S., this family function would involve teaching children to share and to not hurt other children

d.   one way parents accomplish this is by providing and controlling their children's opportunities, such as signing up their daughters for ballet lessons but not for the local soccer team

e.   this notion emphasizes that no family member functions in isolation and that all members are interdependent and reciprocally influence one another

f.   this phenomenon would be demonstrated by a study showing that colic in early infancy causes poor parental responsiveness in late infancy, which in turn causes poor self-regulation in toddlerhood

g.   parents who exhibit this set clear limits for their children but allow their children considerable autonomy within these limits

h.   adolescents have a particularly hard time in families of this type

i.   although parents who exhibit this can be very affectionate, they do not require their children to behave in appropriate ways and thus would be relatively unlikely to intervene if their children hit and kick them in the midst of a temper tantrum

j.   even though parents who exhibit this are likely to use threats and punishment if children do poorly at school, their children tend to be relatively low in academic competence

k.   parental responsiveness and demandingness are two facets of these

l.   parents' poor impulse control and the feeling of being unable to control one's children contribute to this

m.   sending children to school in the U.S. and teaching children how to weave baskets to sell in Columbia are examples of this family function

Multiple-Choice Questions

1. Family dynamics include which of the following?
   A. the influence of parents on children
   B. the influence of children on parents
   C. the influence of siblings on each other
   D. the influence of mother and father on each other
   E. all of the above

2. Which of the following is an example of a parent's direct socialization of modesty?
   A. Abigail (the mother) dresses in reserved clothing.
   B. Judy signs her child up for a class at the local church on growing up with religion.
   C. John explains to his child how important it is to have respect for oneself and one's appearance.
   D. all of the above

3. Parents who are high in warmth and low in control are considered to exhibit which of the following parenting styles?
   A. permissive
   B. authoritative
   C. rejecting-neglecting
   D. authoritarian

4. Authoritative parents are those who:
   A. are abusive.
   B. are highly demanding and unresponsive.
   C. have little interest in disciplining their children.
   D. are attentive, communicative, and consistent in their discipline.

5. Children of which type of parents tend to be low in academic competence and high in impulsive or antisocial behavior (e.g., aggression, drug use)?
   A. permissive
   B. authoritative
   C. rejecting-neglecting
   D. authoritarian
   E. A and C
   F. A and D
   G. C and D

6. Which of the following is <u>not</u> an example of psychological control?
   A. discounting children's feelings
   B. withdrawing love and attention when children behave poorly
   C. threatening children with physical punishment for noncompliance
   D. belittling children's worth

7. Bidirectionality of parent-child interactions refers to the finding that:
   A. children learn to communicate from the reciprocity of early parent-infant babbling.
   B. children's behavior affects parents' behavior, which in turn affects children's behavior.
   C. parents' and children's ethnicity affects their interactions with each other.
   D. parents' genotypes influence both parents' phenotypes and children's genotypes.

8. Imagine that researchers interested in the bidirectional influence of children's compliance with parental requests and parental use of reasoning examined these two variables when a group of children was at each of three ages: two years old, five years old, and eight years old. Which of the following would be support for the bidirectional influence of these variables?
   A. Greater compliance at age two was associated with greater reasoning at age five, which was associated with greater compliance at age eight.
   B. Greater reasoning at age two was associated with less compliance at age five, which was associated with less compliance at age eight.
   C. Greater reasoning at age two was associated with greater reasoning at age five, which was associated with greater compliance at age eight.
   D. Greater compliance at age two was associated with greater compliance at age five, which was associated with greater reasoning at age eight.
   E. All of the above would be support for the bidirectional influence of these variables.

9. Which of the following is a true statement about the association between child maltreatment and family income?
   A. Maltreatment occurs <u>only</u> in poor families.
   B. Maltreatment rates are <u>negatively</u> associated with family income.
   C. Maltreatment rates are <u>unassociated</u> with family income.
   D. Maltreatment rates are <u>positively</u> associated with family income.

10. Compared to parents with less education, parents with more education are more likely to:
   A. view children as active participants in their own development.
   B. allow children to voice opinions about rules and discipline.
   C. be concerned with their children' thoughts and feelings.
   D. all of the above
   E. none of the above

11. In Western industrialized cultures, fathers' play is more likely than mothers' play to include:
   A. reading.
   B. rough-and-tumble play.
   C. teaching.
   D. none of the above

12. Which of the following does <u>not</u> increase the likelihood that siblings will get along?
   A. similarity of siblings' temperaments
   B. preparing older siblings for the arrival of a new sibling
   C. similar treatment by parents
   D. high-quality parental relationship
   E. All of the above increase the likelihood that siblings will get along.

13. Compared to younger mothers, older mothers:
   A. are less satisfied with their role as parents.
   B. have more financial resources.
   C. display less positive emotion with their babies.
   D. B and C
   E. all of the above

14. Which of the following <u>decreases</u> the likelihood that children will experience negative consequences from their parents' divorce?
   A. noncustodial parent permissiveness
   B. custodial parent isolation from social support
   C. authoritarian parenting
   D. low conflict between parents

15. Children of what age are most likely to blame themselves for divorce?
   A. younger children
   B. older children
   C. early adolescents
   D. late adolescents

16. Which of the following is a true statement about children and stepfathers?
   A. Relationships between children and stepfathers tend to be particularly bad in complex stepfamilies.
   B. Conflict between children and biological fathers is more common than conflict between children and stepfathers.
   C. Over time, stepfathers tend to become emotionally distant and disengaged parents.
   D. Stepchildren do not tend to contribute to the conflict with their stepfathers.
   E. A and B
   F. A and C
   G. C and D

17. Which of the following is <u>not</u> a true statement about the adjustment of children of gay and lesbian parents?
   A. The factors involved in adjustment tend to be quite different from the factors involved in the adjustment of children of heterosexual parents.
   B. The adjustment of children of lesbian parents is associated with the extent to which the mother and her partner share child-care duties.
   C. The adjustment of children of gay men is associated with the inclusion of the father's partner in family life.
   D. All of the above are true statements.

18. Which of the following is a true statement about the effects of maternal employment on infants?
   A. There is little evidence that maternal employment has a negative influence on infants.
   B. Part-time maternal employment tends to be worse for infants than full-time maternal employment.
   C. The effects of maternal employment on infants appear to be particularly pronounced for infants whose mothers are not sensitive caregivers.
   D. The effects of maternal employment on infants appear to be limited to infants' social development.

19. The large-scale study of the effects of child care that was funded by the National Institute of Child Health and Development has demonstrated that which of the following is the most important predictor of security of attachment in infancy?
   A. quality of child care
   B. stability of child care
   C. family characteristics
   D. age at which child care began

20. The large-scale study of the effects of child care that was funded by the National Institute of Child Health and Development has demonstrated which of the following about the effects of child care on behavioral problems in children?
   A. The quality of child care is a critical predictor of attachment security.
   B. The amount of child care is a critical predictor of attachment security.
   C. Characteristics of child care were predictive of behavioral problems only when mothers were unresponsive or low in sensitivity.
   D. A and B

Essay Questions

Instructions: Answer the following essay questions on a separate sheet of paper.

1. Describe the family dynamics that may be involved when the mother in the Smith family, made up of a mother and a father and their two young children--Fiona, who is one year old and Gavin, who is three years old--decides to go back to school part time. When the mother is at school two days a week, the children's paternal grandmother (their father's mother) will take care of them. What are some possible effects on how the family operates as a whole, and how might it affect the development of the two children in the family?

2. Describe the child development outcomes that are associated with an authoritarian parenting style and a permissive parenting style. Why do you think each of these parenting styles is associated with these particular outcomes for children?

3. Describe the influences of poverty and homelessness on parenting styles and behaviors. Are any of the parental behaviors that are more common for these children than for other children beneficial for children living in these circumstances? Why or why not?

4. How do you think parents influence children's relationships with their siblings? Be specific and provide supportive examples.

5. What advice can you give to custodial parents and stepparents to increase the likelihood of children adjusting well to living with a stepparent?

Answer Key

Key Term Matching I

1. f	3. g	5. c	7. j	9. h	11. e	13. k
2. l	4. m	6. a	8. d	10. b	12. i	

Key Term Matching II

1. g	3. b	5. d	7. a	9. c	11. i	13. l
2. m	4. e	6. k	8. j	10. f	12. h	

Multiple-Choice Questions

1. E	6. C	11. B	16. F
2. C	7. B	12. E	17. A
3. A	8. A	13. B	18. C
4. D	9. B	14. D	19. C
5. E	10. D	15. A	20. B

CHAPTER 13
Peer Relationships

You Should Know:

Introduction

- what observations Anna Freud and Sophie Dann made of a group of children whose parents had been killed by Hitler and what their conclusions about the importance of peer relationships were.

- what Suomi and Harlow found and how some of their findings with socially isolated monkeys supported Freud's and Dann's observations of children.

What is Special About Peer Relationships? (*summary on pg. 497 of text*)

- what Piaget, Vygotsky, and Sullivan believed was unique to peer relationships and the ways in which peer relationships facilitate children's development.

Friendships (*summary on pg. 508 of text*)

Introduction
- how friendships differ from other peer relationships.

Early Peer Interactions and Friendships
- what evidence supports the existence of friendships in very young children.
- how young children's behavior differs when they are interacting with friends versus nonfriends.

Developmental Changes in Friendship
- how school-age children's behavior differs when they are interacting with friends versus nonfriends.
- how children's conceptions of what a friend is and what is important in a friendship changes from childhood through early adolescence and adolescence.
- what researchers and theorists have claimed accounts for these developmental changes in children's friendship conceptions.

The Functions of Friendships
- how friendships can provide a source of emotional support and understanding for children and how this appears to provide a buffer for children during difficult times.
- how friendships can provide a context for the development of social and cognitive skills.
- how the features of friendships appear to differ between the friendships of girls and those of boys.

Effects of Friendships on Psychological Functioning and Behavior over Time
- what long-term benefits appear to be associated with having friends and why it is difficult to determine the direction of causality.
- how children's aggression and use of alcohol and drugs are associated with the aggression and alcohol and drug use displayed by their friends and why it is difficult to determine the direction of causality.
- which children and adolescents may be most susceptible to the negative influence of friends.

Children's Choice of Friends
- what factors appear to influence with which of their peers children become friends and how these factors change with development.

Box 13.1: Culture and Children's Peer Experience
- how cultural differences in values, expectations, and the structure of society appear to influence the quantity and types of children's interactions with peers.

Peers in Groups *(summary on pg. 512 of text)*

The Nature of Young Children's Groups
- that dominance hierarchies exist even within groups of very young children.

Cliques and Social Networks in Middle Childhood and Early Adolescence
- the features and functions of school-age children's cliques.

Cliques and Social Networks in Adolescence
- how the structure and dynamics of cliques change as children enter preadolescence and adolescence.
- what crowds are and how they may influence adolescents' peer interactions and behaviors.

Boys and Girls in Cliques and Crowds
- how boys' and girls' clique affiliations differ.

Negative Influences of Cliques and Social Networks
- how the members of a clique may influence each others' behaviors in negative ways.
- what features of gangs are common and how gang membership appears to influence adolescents' and young adults' behavior.
- how family and cultural influences appear to play a role in the potential for peer-group promotion of problem behavior.

Status in the Peer Group (*summary on pg. 523 of text*)

Measurement of Peer Status
- how sociometric status is generally measured by researchers.

Characteristics Associated with Sociometric Status
- what factors appear to play a role in how well-liked a child is.
- how children are classified as popular, rejected, neglected, average, and controversial.
- what characteristics and behaviors are common to children in each status group.
- what types of rejected children exist and whether aggressive behavior and withdrawn behavior are always associated with rejection.

Box 13.2: Fostering Children's Peer Acceptance
- what social skills training is and upon what assumption it relies.
- what features are common to social skills training programs.
- the extent to which these intervention programs have been successful.

Stability of Sociometric Status
- the extent to which sociometric status is stable over time and how stability is related to the time period and the status group of interest.

Developmental Trends in Predictors of Children's Sociometric Status
- how the characteristics of popular children change with age.
- how the apparent influence of aggressive and withdrawn behavior on sociometric status changes with age.

Cross-Cultural Similarities and Differences in Factors Related to Peer Status
- what similarities and differences in the behaviors related to peer status have been found cross-culturally and what may account for cultural differences.

Peer Status as a Predictor of Risk
- how peer status is associated with academic performance and long-term adjustment.
- the extent to which we can conclude that a causal path exists between rejection and poor long-term adjustment.

The Role of Parents in Children's Peer Relationships *(summary on pg. 527 of text)*

Relations Between Attachment and Competence with Peers

- the perspective of attachment theorists on the association between parent-child attachment and peer relationships.

- what evidence supports these theoretical views and why this link may exist.

Quality of Ongoing Parent-Child Interactions and Peer Relationships

- how mothers' and fathers' parenting practices are associated with children's peer relationships and why these associations may exist.

- the extent to which we can conclude the existence of a causal relationship between parent-child interactions and children's peer interactions.

Parental Beliefs and Behaviors

- how parents' beliefs about their children's social behaviors and about their own role in children's social behaviors are associated with children's peer interactions.

Gatekeeping, Coaching, and Modeling by Parents

- how parents may influence children's peer relationships through gatekeeping behaviors and by modeling and coaching socially competent behaviors.

Family Stress and Children's Social Competence

- how family economic status is associated with children's peer relations and what may account for this association.

Key Term Matching I: Definitions

Instructions: Match each key term with its definition.

KEY TERM

1. _____ peers
2. _____ crowds
3. _____ victimized peer status
4. _____ social skills training
5. _____ friendships
6. _____ aggressive-rejected children
7. _____ sociometric status
8. _____ withdrawn-rejected children

9. _____ rejected peer status
10. _____ gangs
11. _____ controversial peer status
12. _____ popular peer status
13. _____ cliques
14. _____ neglected peer status
15. _____ relational aggression
16. _____ reciprocated best friendship

DEFINITION

a. a category of sociometric status that includes children who are not particularly liked or disliked by their peers

b. intimate, reciprocated positive relationships between two people

c. a friendship in which two children view one another as best friends

d. friendship groups that children voluntarily join or form themselves

e. groups of adolescents who have similar stereotyped reputations

f. loosely-organized groups of adolescents or young adults that identify as a group and often engage in illegal activities

g. a category of sociometric status that includes children who are liked by few peers and disliked by many peers

h. a category of sociometric status that includes children who are liked by few peers and disliked by many peers <u>and</u> are socially withdrawn and often timid

i. a measurement of the degree to which children are liked or disliked by their peers as a group

j.   a category of sociometric status that includes children who are liked by few peers and disliked by many peers <u>and</u> are especially prone to hostile and physically aggressive behavior

k.   a type of aggression that involves trying to hurt the social relationships of others

l.   a category of sociometric status that includes children who are liked by many peers and disliked by few peers

m.   training programs aimed at teaching rejected children the knowledge and skills that are believed to be associated with positive peer relations

n.   individuals who are of the same age and status

o.   a category of sociometric status that includes children who are liked by a number of peers and disliked by a number of other peers

p.   children in this status group tend to be the targets of their peers' aggression and demeaning behavior

Key Term Matching II: Applications, Examples, and More

Instructions: Match each key term with an application or example of the term.

KEY TERM

1. _____ controversial peer status
2. _____ reciprocated best friendship
3. _____ peers
4. _____ social skills training
5. _____ crowds
6. _____ gangs
7. _____ popular peer status
8. _____ withdrawn-rejected children

9. _____ rejected peer status
10. _____ aggressive-rejected children
11. _____ neglected peer status
12. _____ sociometric status
13. _____ cliques
14. _____ relational aggression
15. _____ friendships

APPLICATION OR EXAMPLE

a. this may involve teaching children strategies they can use in specific peer contexts

b. children in this status group tend to have trouble finding constructive solutions to difficult social situations

c. research has indicated that children who are victimized by their peers do better in terms of adjustment if they have this type of friendship

d. in middle childhood, these tend to include children of the same sex and race

e. children in this status group tend to be cooperative and friendly and to regulate their emotions well

f. 40 to 50% of rejected children tend to fall into this category

g. children may be asked to nominate the children whom they like the most and those whom they like the least in order for researchers to calculate a measure of this for each child in the group

h. "jocks" and "loners" are examples of types of these that are typical among American high school students

i. some evidence suggests that even very young children have these

j. adolescents tend to join these for protection

k.   spreading rumors and excluding peers are examples of this

l.   children who are classified as this tend to exhibit withdrawn behavior coupled with negative actions or emotions

m.   theorists such as Piaget, Vygotsky, and Sullivan have argued that children's relationships with _____ provide a unique context for development

n.   children who are classified as this tend to be both less sociable and less aggressive than average children, but they display relatively few behaviors that differentiate them from other children

o.   children who are classified as this tend to exhibit characteristics of both popular and rejected children

Multiple-Choice Questions

1. Suomi and Harlow's study of isolated monkeys who were then placed with other monkeys demonstrated that:
   A. peer interaction has little impact on the severely abnormal behaviors of previously isolated monkeys.
   B. peers can provide monkeys with some of the social and emotional experiences necessary for normal development.
   C. peers alone can produce optimal development in monkeys.
   D. A and B
   E. B and C

2. As children develop, their friendships:
   A. tend to emphasize closeness and loyalty to a lesser extent.
   B. tend to involve rewards and costs to a greater extent.
   C. are less likely to remain intact following conflict.
   D. all of the above
   E. none of the above

3. Having supportive friends is <u>least</u> likely to be able to help children:
   A. who are experiencing major stressful life experiences.
   B. be less likely to experience loneliness.
   C. who are being victimized by their peers.
   D. as they transition to a new school.
   E. A and C
   F. C and D

4. Which of the following features of friendships tend <u>not</u> to differ between the friendships of elementary school boys and the friendships of elementary school girls?
   A. level of help and guidance
   B. level of intimacy
   C. level of companionship and recreational opportunities
   D. difficulty resolving conflict
   E. all of the above

5. Which of the following does <u>not</u> appear to contribute to cultural differences in children's experience with peers?
   A. educational practices
   B. parents' beliefs about independence
   C. parents' expectations for skills of children of different ages
   D. whether the society is kin-based or not
   E. All of the above influence cultural differences in children's experience with peers.

6. Cliques refer to which of the following?
   A. the friendships of preschool children
   B. friendship groups that children voluntarily form or join
   C. groups of children or adolescents with the same stereotyped reputation
   D. groups of adolescents that often engage in illegal activities
   E. all of the above

7. Which of the following tends to be true of middle childhood friendship cliques?
   A. members are of the same race
   B. include children with great variability on behavioral characteristics
   C. include members of both sexes
   D. all members consider all other members close friends

8. Which of the following is a true statement about girls' and boys' diversity of friends?
   A. Girls have a <u>greater</u> diversity of friends than boys.
   B. Girls have a <u>less</u> diversity of friends than boys.
   C. Girls and boys have <u>similar</u> diversity of friends.
   D. Girls' and boys' diversity of friends differs only prior to adolescence and then becomes more similar.

9. In comparison to adolescents, school-age children:
   A. are more likely to be part of a crowd.
   B. are more likely to belong to multiple cliques.
   C. tend to look more to individual relationships rather than group relationships to fulfill their social needs.
   D. all of the above
   E. none of the above

10. Individuals join and remain in gangs because they provide members with:
   A. a way to spend time.
   B. protection.
   C. a sense of belonging.
   D. all of the above

11. Which of the following decreases children's likelihood of being negatively influenced by the peer group?
   A. authoritarian parenting
   B. living with a stepfather
   C. independence from mother
   D. all of the above
   E. none of the above

12. Neglected children are those who:
   A. are rejected.
   B. have low social impact.
   C. have high social impact.
   D. are aggressive.
   E. A and B
   F. C and D

13. Which of the following is a true statement about the aggression levels of school-age children who are sociometrically popular?
   A. Popular children rarely exhibit aggressive behavior.
   B. Popular children exhibit levels of aggression similar to those of rejected children.
   C. Popular children differ from sociometrically average children in aggression only in terms of aggression that is hostile and angry in nature.
   D. Popular children differ from sociometrically average children in aggression only in terms of aggression that is assertive (such as pushing to get a toy) in nature.
   E. B and C
   F. B and D

14. Which of the following is a true statement about predictors of sociometric status across development?
   A. Withdrawn behavior tends to become a less important predictor of peer <u>rejection</u> as children get older.
   B. Overtly aggressive behavior tends to become a more important predictor of peer <u>rejection</u> as children get older.
   C. The predictors of sociometric <u>popularity</u> tend to remain the same across development.
   D. Adolescents who are labeled as "popular" by their peers tend to exhibit the same behaviors as those who are considered <u>popular</u> by sociometric standards.
   E. all of the above

15. Children who are in which of the following categories in third grade are most likely to experience internalizing symptoms when they are in tenth grade?
   A. popular
   B. controversial
   C. average
   D. aggressive-rejected
   E. All of the above are equally unlikely to experience internalizing symptoms.

16. Which of the following is <u>not</u> likely to be considered indicative of an internalizing symptom?
   A. delinquency
   B. depression
   C. loneliness
   D. obsessive-compulsive behavior

17. Which of the following is a true statement about the long-term adjustment of withdrawn children?
    A. These children tend not to differ from other children once they become adults.
    B. Withdrawn girls, but not boys, tend to have poor long-term adjustment.
    C. Withdrawn boys, but not girls, tend to have poor long-term adjustment.
    D. Both withdrawn boys and withdrawn girls tend to have poor long-term adjustment.

18. Attachment theorists propose that securely attached children will have high quality peer relationships because these children:
    A. have positive social expectations.
    B. tend to be confident and emotionally positive.
    C. understand relationship reciprocity.
    D. all of the above

19. Betsy is a child who has many social difficulties. When she displays aggressive behavior with a peer, her mother is relatively likely to:
    A. believe she should teach Betsy how to handle difficult social situations.
    B. try to organize more opportunities for Betsy to have interaction with peers.
    C. believe the aggressive behavior is part of Betsy's nature.
    D. believe it would be easy to stop Betsy from being aggressive in the future.

20. Which of the following may account for the association between family economic status and children's peer relations?
    A. parental warmth
    B. parental monitoring
    C. prejudice
    D. all of the above

Essay Questions

Instructions: Answer the following essay questions on a separate sheet of paper.

1. Do preschool friends have more or less conflict than preschool nonfriends? Describe how the ways that conflict gets resolved differ between those who are friends and those who are nonfriends.

2. Do you think social interactions, including friendships and associations with cliques are more important to adolescent boys or girls, or are they equally important to adolescents of both sexes? Give examples to support your view.

3. Does researchers' classification of children into the five basic acceptance categories seem accurate to you? Can you think of children you knew growing up who could have been placed into each of these categories? If so, give examples. If not, explain why you cannot place anyone into a particular category. Do you think any categories are inaccurate? Would you add any?

4. Describe the ways in which parents can influence their children's peer interactions through the following three processes: (1) gatekeeping, (2) coaching, and (3) modeling. Be sure to give an example of each. To what extent does the influence of these parental behaviors change with the age of the child?

5. Imagine a school-age child who is having trouble with her peers. She is poorly liked by them, and she has few friends. Which of these two issues do you think is more serious? Why? Be sure to describe the negative outcomes associated with being rejected and with having few or no friends as well as the positive outcomes associated with positive peer relationships.

Answer Key

Key Term Matching I

1. n	4. m	7. i	10. f	13. d	16. c
2. e	5. b	8. h	11. o	14. a	
3. p	6. j	9. g	12. l	15. k	

Key Term Matching II

1. o	4. a	7. e	10. f	13. d
2. c	5. h	8. l	11. n	14. k
3. m	6. j	9. b	12. g	15. i

Multiple-Choice Questions

1. B	6. B	11. E	16. A
2. E	7. A	12. B	17. C
3. A	8. B	13. C	18. D
4. C	9. E	14. C	19. C
5. E	10. D	15. D	20. D

CHAPTER 14
Moral Development

You Should Know:

Moral Judgment (*summary on pg. 544 of text*)

Introduction
- why theorists and researchers have emphasized the reasoning behind a behavior as being critical for determining its morality.

Piaget's Theory of Moral Judgment
- how Piaget studied children's moral development.
- what stages Piaget believed children undergo in the development of morality and what factors he believed contribute to their beliefs in each stage and their advancement from one stage to the next.
- the strengths and weaknesses of Piaget's theory of moral judgment.

Kohlberg's Theory of Moral Judgment
- how Kohlberg examined children's moral development.
- what stages Kohlberg believed individuals undergo in the development of morality, including what types of responses to his moral dilemmas are characteristic of each stage.
- how cognitive development is associated with moral reasoning.
- what major criticisms of Kohlberg's theory have been asserted and what evidence exists to support these criticisms.
- how moral judgment is associated with moral behavior.

Prosocial Moral Judgment
- what types of dilemmas involve prosocial moral judgment.
- what stages of prosocial moral development have been proposed by Eisenberg and how these stages relate to Kohlberg's stages.
- the extent to which the existence of these stages has been supported by research and how cultural differences are believed to influence prosocial moral reasoning.

Domains of Social Judgment
- what types of social judgment exist and when children differentiate among the three domains.
- how cultural and subcultural differences are related to what domain individuals believe particular decisions belong.

The Early Development of Conscience (*summary on pg. 546 of text*)

Introduction

- what the conscience is and how it influences behavior.

Factors Affecting the Development of Conscience

- how parental discipline practices appear to influence the development of children's conscience.
- how individual differences in children are associated with the manner in which children develop a conscience.

Prosocial Behavior (*summary on pg. 555 of text*)

Introduction

- the extent to which prosocial behavior is consistent from childhood into adulthood.

The Development of Prosocial Behavior

- what empathy and sympathy are and how they are relevant to prosocial behavior.
- what factors appear to contribute to children's experiences of empathy and sympathy.
- how prosocial behavior generally develops and what appears to account for this progression.

The Origins of Individual Differences in Prosocial Behavior

- how biological factors likely influence prosocial behavior.
- how parents socialize prosocial behavior and the apparent effectiveness of each manner of socialization.
- how television influences prosocial behavior.

Box 14.1: School-Based Interventions for Promoting Prosocial Behavior

- how the Child Development Project attempted to promote prosocial behavior and how effective it was.
- how caring school community programs have influenced children.

Box 14.2: Cultural Contributions to Children's Prosocial and Antisocial Tendencies

- how cultural values and practices are related to children's prosocial and antisocial behaviors.

Antisocial Behavior (*summary on pg. 567 of text*)

The Development of Aggression and Other Antisocial Behaviors
- how aggression, in terms of quantity, type, and motives, develops during childhood.

Box 14.3: Gender Differences in Prosocial and Antisocial Behavior
- how girls and boys compare in terms of empathy and prevalence of various types of aggression.
- what factors may contribute to these gender differences.

Consistency of Aggressive and Antisocial Behavior
- the extent to which aggressive and antisocial behavior are consistent over time.
- how juvenile delinquency relates to long-term aggression.

Characteristics of Aggressive-Antisocial Children and Adolescents
- what temperamental and personality characteristics are associated with aggression and antisocial behavior.
- how social cognitive factors are associated with aggression and antisocial behavior.

The Origins of Aggression
- how biological factors, family dynamics, and socioeconomic factors appear to contribute to aggression.
- how parenting practices may contribute to aggression and how these associations differ across subcultural groups.
- how friends, the larger peer group, and gangs appear to influence aggressive and antisocial behavior.
- how television and video games contributes to aggressive and antisocial behavior.

Biology and Socialization: Their Joint Influence on Children's Antisocial Behavior
- how biology and socialization appear to interact to contribute to children's aggressive and antisocial behavior.

Box 14.4: The Fast Track Intervention
- the objectives and methodology of the Fast Track Intervention project.
- the extent to which the program has been successful.

Key Term Matching I: Definitions

Instructions: Match each key term with its definition.

KEY TERM

1. _____ empathy
2. _____ proactive aggression
3. _____ prosocial behavior
4. _____ aggression
5. _____ moral judgments
6. _____ altruistic motives
7. _____ social conventional judgments

8. _____ relational aggression
9. _____ personal judgments
10. _____ instrumental aggression
11. _____ sympathy
12. _____ reactive aggression
13. _____ conscience

DEFINITION

a. voluntary behavior intended to benefit another

b. decisions that involve issues of right and wrong, fairness, and justice

c. unemotional aggression aimed at fulfilling a need or desire

d. decisions in which individual preferences are the main consideration

e. emotionally driven, antagonistic aggression

f. aggression motivated by the desire to obtain a concrete goal

g. an emotional reaction to another person's emotional state that is highly consistent with that other person's emotional state

h. the feeling of concern for another person in reaction to that person's emotional state

i. behavior aimed at hurting or injuring others

j. reasons for which individuals help others, including empathy, sympathy, and the desire to act in ways that are consistent with one's conscience and moral standards

k. aggression that harms others by damaging their relationships with peers

l. an internal regulatory mechanism that increases an individual's ability to conform with standards of behavior that are considered acceptable in his or her culture

m. decisions that involve customs or regulations intended to ensure social coordination and social organization

Key Term Matching II: Applications, Examples, and More

Instructions: Match each key term with an application or example of the term.

KEY TERM

1. _____ sympathy
2. _____ relational aggression
3. _____ empathy
4. _____ personal judgments
5. _____ conscience
6. _____ altruistic motives
7. _____ social conventional judgments

8. _____ prosocial behavior
9. _____ proactive aggression
10. _____ instrumental aggression
11. _____ moral judgments
12. _____ reactive aggression
13. _____ aggression

APPLICATION OR EXAMPLE

a. this can promote prosocial behavior by causing a child to feel guilty when he or she engages in unkind behavior

b. even young children understand that transgressions in these types of decisions are wrong even if an adult says they are acceptable

c. parents want children to help others as a result of these rather than as a result of a desire to avoid getting in trouble with parents

d. young children's aggression is generally of this type, as when they push a child so that they can play with a toy they desire

e. examples of this include helping, sharing, and comforting others

f. examples of these include decisions about manners and modes of dress in particular contexts

g. children prone to this are particularly likely to perceive others as possessing hostile motives

h. a child who is worried about another child who is crying is experiencing this

i. this evolves from being almost entirely physical in the early years to involving more verbal forms as children develop

j. adolescents and parents often argue over the issue of whether parents should have any control over these types of decisions

k.   examples of this include spreading negative rumors and excluding a child from a play group

l.   a child who feels sad when she sees another child crying is experiencing this

m.   children prone to this tend to anticipate relatively positive social consequences to their aggression

Multiple-Choice Questions

1. With which of the following statements about morality would cognitive-developmental theorists <u>disagree</u>?
   A. Children actively think about right and wrong.
   B. Social interactions influence children's moral behavior.
   C. A child's moral reasoning changes as a function of cognitive advances.
   D. Children generally learn to behave morally by modeling their parents' behavior.

2. According to Piaget, which of the following is a key factor in children's transition from the morality of constraint to autonomous morality?
   A. parents' requirement for children to not question their rules
   B. the increasing time children spend with peers
   C. children's cognitive immaturity
   D. adults' instructions on the morality and immorality of particular behaviors

3. Which of the following aspects of Piaget's theory of moral reasoning has <u>not</u> been supported by empirical research?
   A. Children whose parents are punitive will make progress in moral reasoning more slowly.
   B. Children's cognitive development plays a role in maturity of moral reasoning.
   C. The amount of time children spend with peers influences the maturity of their moral reasoning.
   D. Older children use intentions and motives to a greater extent than do younger children when determining the morality of a behavior.

4. According to Kohlberg, individuals at the least advanced stage of moral reasoning believe that morally right behavior involves:
   A. upholding laws.
   B. universal principles of justice.
   C. obedience to authorities.
   D. doing what is expected by people close to the individual.

5. Which of the following statements constitutes <u>preconventional</u> moral reasoning?
   A. "I shouldn't do that because it is my responsibility to fulfill my duties."
   B. "I shouldn't do that because I will get caught and I don't want to be punished."
   C. "I shouldn't do that because it is not in the best interest of society."
   D. "I shouldn't do that because my parents won't think I am a good boy."

6. Which of the following is a true statement about the moral reasoning of males and females?
    A. Males and females tend to score similarly on Kohlberg's stages of moral development.
    B. Males tend to score higher than females on Kohlberg's stages of moral development.
    C. Females tend to score higher than males on Kohlberg's stages of moral development.
    D. Although males tend to score more highly than females in adolescence, these differences even out in adulthood.

7. Imagine the following prosocial moral dilemma: "On his way to school, a boy named Freddie sees another boy fall in the mud and start to cry. The boy says he hurt himself and asks Freddie to help him up, but Freddie is worried that if he helps him, he will get himself all muddy. What should Freddie do?" Which of the following responses would be considered the most advanced by Eisenberg?
    A. "Freddie should help because the boy is hurt."
    B. "Freddie should not help because his teacher will think he is bad if he gets to school all dirty."
    C. "Freddie should help because he will feel bad if the boy is hurt and he doesn't help him."
    D. "Freddie should not help the boy because he will get dirty, and he doesn't want to get dirty."

8. Which of the following would be considered by most people in Western cultures to be a moral judgment?
    A. choosing whether or not to wear a tie to a formal restaurant
    B. deciding whether to play soccer or baseball after school
    C. deciding whether to put one's napkin on one's lap or leave it on the table
    D. choosing whether or not to return a $10 bill dropped by a person standing ahead in line

9. Which of the following is a true statement about the domains of social judgment in different cultures?
    A. The distinctions among the three domains in terms of what decisions fall into each category are consistent across cultures.
    B. People in different cultures vary as to which decisions are believed to fall into each category.
    C. Any differences across cultures in terms of the domains of social judgment are a result of cultural differences in level of education.
    D. People in some cultures do not differentiate among the three domains of social judgment.
    E. B and C

10. What should parents pay attention to when disciplining their children if their goal is for their children to internalize parental standards for behavior?
    A. ensuring the discipline is not so harsh as to cause high levels of distress in children who will then tune out their parents' message
    B. ensuring that the discipline is not so gentle as to not sufficiently arouse the child's attention
    C. both A and B
    D. neither A nor B

11. An emotional reaction to another's emotional state that is similar to the other person's emotional state is referred to as:
  A. altruism.
  B. sympathy.
  C. conscience.
  D. empathy.

12. Results of a twin study designed to estimate the contribution of genetic factors to children's concern for others and prosocial behavior demonstrated that genetic factors make what type of contribution?
  A. no contribution
  B. very slight contribution
  C. modest contribution
  D. large contribution

13. What is the best strategy for parents to encourage children to behave in a prosocial manner?
  A. point out the consequences of prosocial actions for others
  B. point out that the child has upset the parent when he or she doesn't help others
  C. tell children that prosocial behaviors are good and nice
  D. A and C
  E. all of the above

14. Which of the following parenting practices or styles is associated with increased prosocial behavior in children?
  A. encouraging children to sympathize with others
  B. threatening children for failing to behave prosocially
  C. rewarding children for prosocial behavior
  D. A and C
  E. B and C

15. Aggression that is motivated by the desire to obtain an object or concrete goal is referred to as:
  A. physical aggression.
  B. relational aggression.
  C. instrumental aggression.
  D. antisocial aggression.

16. Which of the following is <u>not</u> a characteristic exhibited by infants and preschoolers who later exhibit a high degree of aggressive and antisocial behavior?
   A. difficult temperament
   B. impulsivity
   C. demanding of attention
   D. irritability
   E. None of the above characteristics is exhibited by infants and preschoolers who later exhibit a high degree of aggressive and antisocial behavior.
   F. All of the above are characteristics exhibited by infants and preschoolers who later exhibit a high degree of aggressive and antisocial behavior.

17. In terms of their social cognition when faced with a negative social situation, aggressive children differ from nonaggressive children in which of the following?
   A. attributions
   B. goals
   C. behavioral options
   D. expectations of the effectiveness of strategies
   E. all of the above

18. Which of the following would be the <u>weakest</u> evidence for a biological influence on aggression?
   A. Testosterone levels are associated with responses to provocation.
   B. Twin studies demonstrate that antisocial behavior runs in families.
   C. Many children engage in delinquency at around the same age – adolescence.
   D. Neurological deficits that affect attention may contribute to antisocial behavior.

19. Which of the following is a true statement about the relation between parents' use of <u>abusive punishment</u> and children's antisocial behavior for African-American and Euro-American children?
   A. Parents' use of abusive punishment is associated with children's antisocial behavior for <u>both</u> African-American and Euro-American children.
   B. Parents' use of abusive punishment is associated with children's antisocial behavior for <u>neither</u> African-American nor Euro-American children.
   C. Parents' use of abusive punishment is associated with children's antisocial behavior for <u>African-American</u> children but not for Euro-American children.
   D. Parents' use of abusive punishment is associated with children's antisocial behavior for <u>Euro-American</u> children but not for African-American children.

20. Which of the following parenting behaviors is <u>not</u> associated with increased antisocial behavior in children?
   A. concessions to children's demands
   B. inconsistent punishing
   C. marital violence
   D. high levels of monitoring
   E. A and B
   F. A and D

Essay Questions

Instructions: Answer the following essay questions on a separate sheet of paper.

1. Describe two similarities and two differences between Piaget's and Kohlberg's theories of moral reasoning. Which theory do you agree with to a greater extent, and why?

2. Describe the pattern of developmental changes in children's prosocial moral reasoning. Give examples where necessary.

3. Describe how sociocultural factors may influence children's understanding of and differentiation among moral, social conventional, and personal judgments. Be specific and provide relevant examples.

4. Are young children capable of taking others' perspectives and experiencing empathy and sympathy? Are they able to engage in altruistic behavior? Provide examples to support your position.

5. Describe the association between parental discipline practices and children's antisocial and aggressive behavior. Be sure to describe the factors that are associated with these behaviors in children, as well as the reasoning for why these associations exist.

Answer Key

Key Term Matching I

1. g	3. a	5. b	7. m	9. d	11. h	13. l
2. c	4. i	6. j	8. k	10. f	12. e	

Key Term Matching II

1. h	3. l	5. a	7. f	9. m	11. b	13. i
2. k	4. j	6. c	8. e	10. d	12. g	

Multiple-Choice Questions

1. D	6. A	11. D	16. F
2. B	7. C	12. C	17. E
3. C	8. D	13. A	18. C
4. C	9. B	14. A	19. A
5. B	10. C	15. C	20. D

CHAPTER 15
Conclusions

You Should Know:

Theme 1: Nature and Nurture: All Interactions, All the Time

Nature and Nurture Begin Interacting Before Birth
- how prenatal development involves not only nature, but nurture and the interaction between the two as well.
- how teratogenic effects and fetal learning are good examples of this concept.

Infants' Nature Elicits Nurture
- how infants' biological characteristics influence their environments.

Timing Matters
- how the nature of the individual at the time of an environmental event can influence the impact of the event.
- how sensitive or critical periods are good examples of this concept.

Nature Does Not Reveal Itself All at Once
- how the influence of genetics does not stop at birth.
- how the development of schizophrenia is a good example of this concept.

Everything Influences Everything
- the extent to which the statement "Everything influences everything else" is accurate and why this is the case.

Theme 2: Children Play Active Roles in Their Own Development

Self-Initiated Activity
- how self-initiated activity, including self-locomotion, contributes to children's development.

Active Interpretation of Experience
- how children's attempts to understand the world and their subjective interpretations of their experiences influence their development.

Self-Regulation
- how children's regulation of their emotions, behavior, activities, etc. contributes to their development.

Eliciting Reactions from Other People
- how children elicit the behaviors of their parents and peers.
- how the negative cycles sometimes experienced by adolescents and their parents are good examples of this concept.

Theme 3: Development Is Both Continuous and Discontinuous

Continuity/Discontinuity of Individual Differences
- how continuous individual differences tend to be over time.
- what accounts for the continuity of individual differences.

Continuity/Discontinuity over Age: The Question of Stages
- the assumptions of stage theories.
- the extent to which stage theories can accurately capture development.
- how one's focus influences whether development appears to be continuous or discontinuous.

Theme 4: Mechanisms of Developmental Change

Biological Change Mechanisms
- how brain development illustrates the complexity of change at the biological level.

Behavioral Change Mechanisms
- how behavioral change mechanisms, including both basic learning mechanisms and social learning, facilitate learning.
- some examples of each of these behavioral change mechanisms.

Cognitive Change Mechanisms
- how general information-processing mechanisms and domain-specific learning mechanisms facilitate developmental change.
- examples of each of these cognitive change mechanisms.

Theme 5: The Sociocultural Context Shapes Development

Growing Up in Societies with Different Values
- how cultural values and practices can underlie a variety of variations across cultures, even in areas that would appear to be biological, such as rate of development.
- the ways in which cultural values exert their influence and some examples of these modes of influence.

Growing Up in Different Times and Places
- how historical changes influence children's development.

Growing Up in Different Circumstances Within a Society
- how differences in economic circumstances, family relationships, and peer groups can lead to differences in children's development, even for children growing up in the same time and place.

Theme 6: How So Children Become So Different from One Another?

Introduction
- what three properties are important in determining whether a dimension of individual differences is considered important.

Breadth of Individual Differences at a Given Time
- what types of individual differences are associated with a broad range of other variables.

Stability over Time
- how the stability of genes and the stability of environment contributes to the stability of many individual differences.

Predicting Future Individual Differences on Other Dimensions
- what contributes to the long-term relations between some individual differences and other important variables.

Determinants of Individual Differences
- the extent to which genes contribute to differences among individuals and how the influence of genetics changes over the course of development.
- the extent to which experience contributes to differences among individuals.

Theme 7: Child-Development Research Can Improve Children's Lives

Implications for Parenting

- what principles of good parenting are suggested by developmental theory and research.

Educational Implications

- what principles of good education are suggested by the four major theories of cognitive development.

Helping Children at Risk

- what principles are suggested for helping children at risk for developmental problems.
- some examples of these principles at work.

Improving Social Policy

- how knowledge of developmental research can help us make better-informed decisions about a variety of social policy issues.
- some examples of the impact of research on policy.

Multiple-Choice Questions

1. Which of the following is an example of the interplay between nature and nurture before birth?
   A. The genetics of the fetus partially determines the effect of teratogens on prenatal development.
   B. The hormones released by the fetus change the prenatal environment, which then influences the fetus.
   C. The food that the mother eats while pregnant influences newborn taste preferences.
   D. all of the above

2. Which of the following is <u>not</u> an example of a self-initiated activity that allows children to actively influence their environment?
   A. language
   B. walking
   C. attractiveness
   D. looking preferences
   E. taste preferences

3. Focusing on which of the following generally makes development appear more continuous?
   A. specific tasks and processes rather than broad domains
   B. behaviors rather than underlying processes
   C. smaller time frames rather than larger time frames
   D. A and C
   E. all of the above
   F. none of the above

4. Which of the following is <u>not</u> a mechanism of developmental change?
   A. history
   B. biology
   C. social learning
   D. automatization of mental processes

5. Japanese culture's value on hiding negative emotions could play a role in differences between U.S. and Japanese children's:
   A. peer relations.
   B. emotional regulation.
   C. moral development.
   D. aggression.
   E. all of the above

6. Which of the following is <u>not</u> a key reason why social competence is considered an important individual difference?
   A. Socially competent children tend to become socially competent adolescents who tend to become socially competent adults.
   B. Social competence in childhood predicts future outcomes, such as self esteem.
   C. Social competence has its basis in genetics.
   D. Social competence has a variety of concurrent associations, such as the number of friends a child has.
   E. All of the above are key reasons why social competence is considered an important individual difference.

7. Which of the following is <u>not</u> a valid conclusion to be drawn from this course when thinking about the implications of developmental psychology for education and social policy?
   A. Most developmental problems stem from one major source, so it is important that we find that source before intervening with children.
   B. Timing of interventions is crucial; in general, the earlier children receive help, the more successful the outcome.
   C. Designing treatments for undesirable behavior is best done by attending to both the biological and environmental factors that are involved.
   D. all of the above
   E. none of the above

Essay Questions

Instructions: Answer the following essay questions on a separate sheet of paper.

1. Choose a domain of development – cognitive, moral, social, language, physical, etc. – and describe three ways in which development in this domain is continuous and three ways in which it is discontinuous. Do the specifics of what you are focusing on change your perception as to whether development in the domain is generally continuous or generally discontinuous?

2. Thinking about the extent to which many individual differences remain stable over time, describe three reasons why self-esteem demonstrates high stability over time. Be sure to provide examples of each.

3. Describe three ways in which children's self-initiated activity actively influences their environment. Be sure to provide examples of each.

4. Think about your own childhood, the development of a particular trait, or your parents' parenting practices. Describe three things you have learned in this course that have influenced your perceptions or memories.

Answer Key

Multiple-Choice Questions

1. D   5. E
2. C   6. C
3. F   7. A
4. A